RUDOLF STEINER (1861–1925) called his spiritual philosophy 'anthroposophy', meaning 'wisdom of the human being'. As a highly developed seer, he based his work on direct knowledge and perception of spiritual dimensions. He initiated a modern and universal 'science of spirit', accessible to anyone willing to exercise clear and unprejudiced thinking.

From his spiritual investigations Steiner provided suggestions for the renewal of many activities, including education (both general and special), agriculture, medicine, economics, architecture, science, philosophy, religion and the arts. Today there are thousands of schools, clinics, farms and other organizations involved in practical work based on his principles. His many published works feature his research into the spiritual nature of the human being, the evolution of the world and humanity, and methods of personal development. Steiner wrote some 30 books and delivered over 6,000 lectures across Europe. In 1924 he founded the General Anthroposophical Society, which today has branches throughout the world.

# THE INTERIOR OF THE EARTH

## An Esoteric Study of the Subterranean Spheres

RUDOLF STEINER

*Compiled and edited by Paul V. O'Leary*

RUDOLF STEINER PRESS

Rudolf Steiner Press
Hillside House, The Square
Forest Row, RH18 5ES

www.rudolfsteinerpress.com

Published by Rudolf Steiner Press 2006

Earlier English publications: See Sources section on p. 127

Originally published in German in various volumes of the GA (*Rudolf Steiner Gesamtausgabe* or Collected Works) by Rudolf Steiner Verlag, Dornach. For further information see Sources, p. 127. This authorized translation is published by permission of the Rudolf Steiner Nachlassverwaltung, Dornach. 'Esoteric Conversations' reproduced by kind permission of Temple Lodge Publishing, Sussex

All material has been translated or checked and revised against the original German by Paul V. O'Leary

A catalogue record for this book is available from the British Library

ISBN-10: 1 85584 119 3
ISBN-13: 978 185584 119 2

Cover by Andrew Morgan Design
Typeset by DP Photosetting, Neath, West Glamorgan
Printed and bound by 4edge Limited, UK

# Contents

# *Foreword*

This volume presents a special selection of lectures and essays by Rudolf Steiner that have a unique place within the massive body of work produced over the course of his life. This publication of material about the interior of the earth arose organically from the first English publication of Sigismund von Gleich's *The Transformation of Evil and the Subterranean Spheres of the Earth.* [1] Readers of that work enquired about von Gleich's sources: lectures of Rudolf Steiner which were scattered in various books, some of which are out of print. They also asked whether additional materials on the same theme existed written either by Steiner or by students of spiritual science. Such are few and far between in anthroposophical literature in English or in German. This book contains ten relevant pieces by Steiner and two by pupils of his, gathered together in a single volume for the first time.

The first section of this book offers, in chronological order, those lectures and lecture excerpts where Steiner discussed the forces active in the interior of the earth. The first four lectures outline in schematic form the essential characteristics of the nine chthonic regions known as the Subterranean Spheres.

Steiner's first public mention of the Subterranean Spheres occurred on 16 April 1906, shortly after the eruption of Mount Vesuvius on 6 April of that year. He emphasized that no one had ever publicly done so, 'not even within the theosophical movement'. Thus, the publication of this collection on the one-hundredth anniversary of its delivery seems quite fitting. His last complete description of all nine regions took place less than five months later, on 4 September 1906. Steiner's only other lecture which speaks directly about this—on 1 January 1909—covered only the first six layers, stopping at the Fire Earth. Otherwise, he never expressly lectured on the topic again.

To observe that this material is difficult only repeats what Steiner himself noted on several occasions: '... even among occultists it is considered one of the most difficult things to speak about the mysterious configuration and composition of our planet earth'. And further: 'These things are part of the most advanced knowledge in occultism'.[2] Present-day humanity '... would really be surprised, perhaps even confused, if they succeeded in learning more about the deeper layers of our earth. They would be confused because they would find things that show only the faintest similarity to what we know upon the earth's surface'.[3]

After these preliminary words of caution Steiner set forth concepts about and descriptions of the subterranean realm which were beyond the experience of the overwhelming majority of his tiny audience in pre-First-World-War Europe, and likely remain so today. Parts of these read like science fiction.

Five additional lecture excerpts are from volumes widely divergent in their subject matter: *Manifestations of Karma* (1910), *Man and the World of Stars* (1922), *Karmic Relationships* Vol. II (1924), and two Leading Letters from *The Michael Mystery*[4] (1925), Steiner's last work before his death in March 1925. Yet, they cover topics intimately connected with the inner earth, including volcanoes, earthquakes and meteorological phenomena. Thus, the material presented here almost spans Steiner's entire public career (1900–1925). The appearance of themes related to the interior of the earth at the end of his life in some of his most important writings bears witness to the importance he placed upon the subject vis-à-vis his entire spiritual-scientific worldview. While the first five lectures set forth a conceptual framework for understanding the Subterranean Spheres, his last two essays read more as a call to action.

Steiner's silence on the topic prompted one of his closest pupils, Adolf Arenson, to author the monograph *The Interior of the Earth* under his guidance. That Steiner provided his closest pupils with more intimate instruction about the interior of the earth is evidenced by his private conversations with Countess Johanna von Keyserlingk, relevant portions of which, along with Arenson's work, are found in the final section of this book.

The majority of Steiner's writings about the development of higher levels of spiritual awareness involve meticulous expositions about the stages of Imagination, Inspiration, Intuition and beyond. These enhanced modes of perception, made possible by the transformation of thinking through concentration, meditation and personal moral development, form the backbone of most courses of study for students of spiritual science. *Knowledge of the Higher Worlds and Its Attainment* is the principal manual, although the path to higher awareness is discussed in literally dozens of other works, including *Occult Science* and *Theosophy*, both considered among anthroposophy's five basic books.[5]

The four 1906 lectures on the Subterranean Spheres featured here—and the relevant portion of the fifth lecture given on 1 January 1909—are the only guides Steiner gave to the world beneath our feet. He presents the other side of the coin, so to speak, fills in the other half of a picture of mankind, based on a spiritual-scientific world conception showing that while human beings are created by the spiritual worlds above them, from the top down, they are also made from polaric forces below them from the bottom up. Subterranean regions are described which live within our subconscious and which consist of pure animal urges and passions, chaos, discord, destruction, hatred and, ultimately, a realm of spiritual evil—the source of black magic. However, these lectures make it clear that 'human evolution implies a transformation of the earth's interior'. Personal (human) evolution and terrestrial evolution are halves of the same whole. 'So the will of human beings is connected with what happens on earth. One transforms one's dwelling place and one's self at the same time. When a person spiritualizes himself, he spiritualizes the earth as well.'[6] The path of Christian esoteric development follows the path of Christ, as each stage of the Passion (the Washing of the Feet, the Scourging, the Crowning with Thorns, etc.) results in the transformation of a corresponding sphere within the interior of the earth. As Steiner advised in his last essay, a balanced pursuit of higher forms of cognition requires the penetration and transformation of these realms. We should advance no higher into the heights of super-consciousness than we have penetrated into the chthonic realms of the Subterranean Spheres. In this manner our feet are kept on the ground and common sense is never lost. To do otherwise is to endanger the soul through imbalances which promote luciferic self-illusion and/or the ahrimanic will-to-power. Thus, these lectures have profound and far-reaching ramifications for students of spiritual science who hope to achieve a comprehensive and modern view of mankind and the world.

*Adolf Arenson*

Adolf Arenson (1855–1936) was among the most prominent figures in the anthroposophical movement prior to the First World War. He was on the executive committee of the German section of the Theosophical Society between 1904 and 1913. He became an esoteric student of Steiner's in 1904 and from 1906 was active as a leader of the esoteric group in Stuttgart. A gifted musician, he composed several operas and also wrote the music for the performances of Edouard Schuré's drama *The Children of Lucifer* (1909) and Steiner's four *Mystery Plays* (1910–1913). He compiled the first reference guide describing the fifty principal lecture-cycles of Rudolf Steiner and was pivotal in the Anthroposophical Society's activities in Stuttgart, Germany. His 1913 lecture 'The Interior of the Earth' was first published in 1914.

*Countess Johanna von Keyserlingk*

The Count and Countess Keyserlingk sponsored the Agricultural Course given by Rudolf Steiner (7–16 June 1924) on their estate in the Silesian village of Koberwitz near Breslau, Germany (now Wroclaw, Poland). The countess was an esoteric pupil of Steiner's and several volumes of her writings were published posthumously (in German). The selected excerpt from 'Esoteric Conversations' is part of her account of the Agricultural Course entitled 'Twelve Days with Rudolf Steiner' found in *The Birth of a New Agriculture: Koberwitz 1924*.[7]

Paul V. O'Leary
2006

# I

# THE INTERIOR OF THE EARTH: A CONCEPTUAL FRAMEWORK

# The Interior of the Earth and Volcanic Eruptions (excerpt)

16 April 1906

As announced, today's lecture will be concerned with a tragic event that happened in these days—the eruption of Mount Vesuvius. It will not be possible to discuss the details of this event of nature. Our task is to awaken insight into such natural phenomena through spiritual science. Let me, therefore, present some basic elements that will make such insight possible. We should note in advance that even among occultists it is considered one of the most difficult things to speak about the mysterious configuration and composition of our planet earth. It is a well known fact—anyone who is even a little informed on occult subjects will have heard this—that it is easier to gain a living experience of the astral and mental worlds, of kamaloka and devachan, and to bring it to ordinary day-consciousness than it is to penetrate the secrets of our own planet earth. In point of fact, these secrets are among the 'inner secrets' which are reserved for a higher grade, the second grade, of initiation. No one has, to date, spoken in public about the interior of the earth, not even within the theosophical movement. I would, therefore, stress at the outset that today's lecture is definitely not for people who are new to theosophy. This is not because there may be difficulties as regards purely conceptual understanding—the content may, in fact, be easier to understand than many other things—but because someone who does not have sufficient knowledge of the research methods used in spiritual science will immediately ask: 'How do you know all this?' I will provide a rough outline of the facts and at the same time indicate the ways in which these matters can be investigated. There will, no doubt, be members of the audience who are not used to hearing unusual things, so that what I am going to say today may seem fantastic. Please remember that we can never understand everything. These things are part of the most advanced knowledge in occultism.

It will thus be necessary for me to speak about the interior of the earth from the occult point of view. As you know, scientists offer very little information. New theories about the origin of volcanoes, and on volcanic activity in general, have come up roughly every five years in recent decades. What I am going to say today will be pushed aside by modern scientists with a wave of the hand as something which has nothing to do with science. By way of introduction, let me show you how this objection appears to occultists.

External science considers that its task is to explain the devastating eruptions from the interior of the earth and the terrifying quakes, which destroy thousands upon thousands of human lives, in purely mechanical terms. One theory is that the interior of the earth consists of red-hot liquid matter, more or less like an overheated stove. Another theory sees that the origin of volcanic phenomena lie in hot spots near the surface which do not penetrate deeply into the earth's interior. More recent theories tend to take this second line. You can hear what modern science has to say in popular science lectures, or read about them in a literature that varies in quality.

The objections raised by geophysicists to the kind of approach we use here may be compared with an ordinary, everyday event. Let us assume that someone has his room furnished by someone else who wanted to do something nice for him. A third person might come and speak of the loving care given to the choice of the different pieces of furniture, how he had followed particular ideas, and so on. But another person might object: 'Why should there be any underlying ideas? The pieces were made at a cabinetmakers and are therefore his work'. Both people are right: the person who speaks about the way the cabinetmaker made the furniture, and the other person who knows what was in the person's heart and mind who gave the furniture and commissioned the cabinetmaker to make it. Scientists are quite right from their point of view. But they should be able to admit that it is possible to have two completely different points of view. We are definitely not interested in rejecting the cabinetmaker-insights of modern science. What matters to us is to reveal the ideas about how everything was created and brought into existence. That is the spiritual aspect.

Let me now speak about the interior of the earth without further ado. This can only be done schematically. As you can imagine, the interior of the earth always looks a little different, depending on where we are on the surface when we consider it. Thus, only a schematic description is possible. To the spiritual scientist the earth is far from being the dead product modern science presents it to be. It is alive and filled with soul and spirit, as the human body is not merely what anatomists show it to be. As the human body is filled with soul and spirit, so is the whole body of the earth filled with soul and spirit. And just as the blood consists not only of the chemical compounds chemists are able to identify, so specific substances and layers in our earth are far from being only what metallurgists, crystallographers and chemists are able to discover. Just as the nerves are not merely the anatomical structures defined by scientists, having special significance in expressing soul qualities, so too, there is an aspect of soul and spirit to everything that makes up our earth.

Physicists are only able to penetrate a short distance towards the interior of the earth. The few thousand metres they are able to reach are of little significance. Scientists only deal with the outermost shell of the earth's body. No such limits are placed upon clairvoyant research when it explores the body of our earth, whereby it is actually possible to penetrate to the centre of the planet. Clairvoyant research also finds that the earth is made up of layers—layers which reveal themselves to perception in stages.

Any of you who have heard the lectures on the Gospel of St John will remember that there are seven stages of Christian initiation. They are:

1. The Washing of the Feet;
2. the Scourging;
3. the Crowning with Thorns;
4. the Carrying of the Cross;
5. the Mystic Death;
6. the Entombment or Burial;
7. the Resurrection.

Something truly remarkable emerges from each stage of initiation in relation to the scientific investigation of the earth. A further, deeper layer of our earth becomes transparent at each stage. Whoever has reached the first stage of initiation can penetrate the first layer of the earth. Whoever has reached the second stage penetrates to the second layer, which looks very different. One who has borne the Crown of Thorns sees the third layer. Then comes the stage of Cross-Bearing, when the fourth layer becomes visible. The fifth stage, Mystic Death, opens up a further layer. There follows the sixth stage, that of Entombment. The seventh layer corresponds to the Resurrection. Thus, there are seven consecutive layers. Beyond these seven, which are the levels a person reaches in going through these seven stages of initiation, lie two more layers—an eighth and a ninth layer. The inner earth therefore consists of nine layers. I have made them all more or less the same width in the drawing [below], although in reality they vary in thickness. The thickness of the layers is of less interest to us today, however.

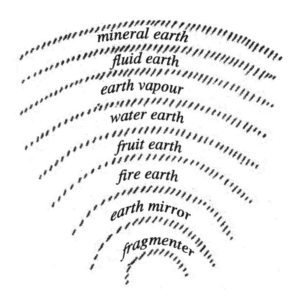

mineral earth
fluid earth
earth vapour
water earth
fruit earth
fire earth
earth mirror
fragmenter

Let us try to describe those nine consecutive layers a little more. The upper layer is the one which contains all the things to which modern science is limited, everything which exists as solid rock or the materials for solid rock.

Then comes the second layer. It differs from the one above

it mainly in that it is in a relatively soft, fluid state. Everything is of such a nature that occultists call it the Fluid or Soft Earth. The outer layer is called Solid or Mineral Earth. The second layer contains things which ordinary physics cannot tell us about, for it is not possible for the time being to create conditions on the earth's surface where the type of substance found in this layer can actually exist. It cannot be found on the earth's surface because it requires the tremendous pressure of the upper layer to hold everything in the second layer together. If you were to take the upper layer away, the material beneath would rush out and spread out into the whole universe with incredible speed. That is the second layer.

The third layer is called the Vapour Earth or Steam Earth. It is more difficult to characterize than the second. You might think of water vapour. Apart from its vaporous state it is also full of life. So we have here a layer which has life, whereas the other two, the first and second layers, do not actually have life. All of the second layer has a tremendous potential for expansion, to shatter apart. The third layer, on the other hand, has life present at every point.

The fourth stratum is so constituted that it no longer has the substantiality we find on the earth, as is found in everything in the three layers above it, which still have more or less something of the nature of our ordinary matter. The substances in this layer cannot be perceived with the outer senses since they are in an astral state. Everything which exists in the three uppermost layers, and is still in a way related to the things we have on the earth's surface, is here found in an astral state. In biblical terms we can say: 'The spirit of God moved upon the waters'. Let us call it the Water Earth, which is also the occult term. The Water Earth is also the origin and source of all matter on earth, all outer matter, irrespective of whether it is found in minerals, plants, animals or human beings. Matter, which is found in everything on our earth, is in a volatile, astral state in the Water Earth. You must realize that everything we have by way of physical forces originates in astral forces, and that these original astral forces condense and become physical. These primal forces exist in the fourth layer, the Water Earth.

The fifth layer is called the Fruit Earth, and is so named for a quite specific reason. Scientists or people in general will ask: 'How did life originate?' This is frequently a topic of discussion not only in popular lectures but also in scientific literature. But you have to be a real dilettante in the realm of spiritual science to ask this question. Such a question simply does not arise in spiritual science; the only question is: 'How has dead matter come about?' I have tried to explain this to you before using an analogy. Look at pit coal—it is simply rock now. Yet, if you were able to trace it back through several millennia of earth's evolution you would find that that piece of coal comes from vast forests of ferns which have turned into coal. What, then, is a coal pit? The coal pit developed from entire forests. Dead today, it once was completely alive.

If you were able to look at the bottom of the ocean you would find all kinds of calcareous formations. Look at marine creatures and you will see that they constantly secrete lime, calcium carbonate. The calcareous shell remains behind as solid matter. Once again you have something dead which is the product of something living. If you had developed supersensible organs of perception and were able to go back far enough in earth evolution, you would find that everything dead comes from something living, and that even rock

crystals and diamonds derive from life. Fossil development in
outer nature is a process similar to the development of the
skeletal system in us. You know that there are fish which have
no bony skeleton. In earlier stages of man you would also find
no bones, only cartilage. Everything which is part of the
skeleton is the beginning of lifelessness in man. It is the same
condensation process.

You should think of the earth's living body in the same
way, as one great living organism. The proper question to ask
is: 'How did dead, lifeless matter, come about?' To ask how
the living came from the dead is one of the silliest questions,
for life came first, and dead matter separated from it in fos-
sils, in a hardening process. At one time life existed
throughout the whole earth. The life which existed then,
when there was as yet no dead matter, was living matter,
which is still found in the Fruit Earth. It just does not have
life which is similar to our present life, like the things we
spoke about earlier. In the Fruit Earth we find life in its most
original state, which was also found on the earth's surface
when nothing lifeless had yet developed. That is how we
should picture the fifth layer, the Fruit Earth.

The sixth layer is the Fire Earth. Just as the Fruit Earth
contains all that lives, so the Fire Earth comprises everything
that exists as drives or instincts. It contains the original
sources of all animal life, life that experiences pleasure and
pain. You may think it strange, but it is true that the Fire
Earth becomes sentient as soon as it expands. This can be
observed. It is a truly sentient layer of the earth. Everything
which exists on earth and which once filled the whole earth is
found in specific layers within the earth. Just as dead matter
comes from life, so does everything which has life come from
the soul sphere. Anything that has life does not come from

anything corporeal. Sentience, soul quality, comes first, and what is bodily arises from it. All matter can be traced back to soul substance.

The seventh layer is called the Mirror Earth or Reflector Earth, and for a very special reason. One unfamiliar with the 'seven unutterable secrets of occultism', as they are called, would find the content of this seventh layer to be grotesque. It contains all the forces of nature, but transformed as spirit. Let me try to explain it like this. Think of magnetism, electricity, heat, light or any force of nature, but transformed into something spiritual. For example, a magnet attracts iron, which is an inorganic effect. Now think of it in spiritual terms, as if the magnet were attracting the iron out of inner sympathy. Think of electrical wires transformed into something spiritual and moral, as if the forces of nature were not mechanical, indifferent forces but worked morally. Think of the forces of heat, repulsion and attraction with soul and moral qualities, as if they wanted to do something nice for people and on that account had an inner feeling about it. First, imagine the whole of nature in moral terms. And then think of the whole of nature as something immoral. Think of everything you can imagine by way of morality in human nature, but turned into its opposite. This is what is found in the Mirror Earth. There is nothing there of what we on earth call 'The Good'. Quite the opposite. The activities most powerful there are the opposite of what people call 'good'. Such are the qualities of this layer. Originally the earth had a great deal more of them, but they are gradually improving as morality progressively develops. The moral development of our earth means that the forces in the Mirror Earth will completely change from being immoral to being moral. The moral process in human society has significance not only for society itself but for the whole planet. It comes to expression in the way the forces of this layer change into moral forces of nature. When our human race has progressed so far that it has produced the highest morality, then everything anti-moral in the Mirror Earth will be overcome and transformed into something moral. That is the purpose of the seventh layer.

The eighth stratum of the interior of the earth has various names. In the Pythagorean School[1] of antiquity it was called the Number Generator. In the Rosicrucian school it was called the Fragmenter or Splinterer. This eighth layer, which consists of a number of forces, has a most peculiar property that can only be discovered in a very strange way. When the spiritual pupil has reached the stage in Christian initiation which is only reached after the stage of Resurrection, he must do the following if he is to get any idea at all of what is happening here. He must take a flower, for example, and visualize it very clearly in his mind's eye. Then he must concentrate on this part of the inner earth in such a way as if he were looking at it through the flower. Everything would then be seen a hundred and a thousandfold through the flower—hence the name Fragmenter. If you took a formless object, like a piece of wood, this would not happen. But if you take a plant, an animal or even a human being, they would appear in countless numbers. A work of art would also be multiplied many times in this way. Not formless matter, but any work of art, provided it is substantial, is multiplied many times. This is peculiar to this layer, which is why it is called the Fragmenter, or in the Pythagorean School, the Number Generator, the latter because it shows things which exist as single objects on earth multiplied many times over.

Then comes the ninth layer which lies immediately around

the earth's centre. This is extremely difficult to penetrate for people today, even for someone advanced in spiritual training. One can only say that one becomes aware how specific parts of the interior of the earth have a certain relationship to individual organs of human and animal bodies. Above all you find forces which have been moved to the periphery, forces whose mode of action is difficult to describe. They stand in a living connection with the human brain, and further inwards, with human brain functions. Still further inside this sphere are forces connected with human and animal powers of reproduction.

So here we have the configuration of our earth as seen with clairvoyant vision and as taught in all occult schools ever since such schools have existed. What you see drawn on the board here is a mystery which is actually taught in all occult schools.

All kinds of connections exist between the individual layers, just as individual organs of the human body are linked in many different ways by blood and nerves. Connecting links go from the centre of the earth in all kinds of directions. Forces move above all in two directions: they pass directly through the centre of the earth and exactly at right angles to each other; they are not strands but are the directions where the forces move. Many other directions may also be noted. The following is important when looking at these things. When we explore the uppermost layer we find it is interrupted by a hollow space that lies inside this outermost layer. A kind of canal links this hollow space with the fifth layer which we call the Fruit Earth.

A natural disaster such as a volcanic eruption involves the deeper layers of the earth, which I have drawn for you. This is true with both volcanic eruptions and earthquakes. The uppermost layers are set in motion by forces that go from the Fruit Earth to the hollow space I have mentioned. These forces essentially arise in the fifth layer of the inner earth. The Fire Earth is also involved, since it is disturbed. The Fire Earth is actually always in a state of unrest, but it becomes particularly restless when abnormal phenomena such as earthquakes or volcanic eruptions occur. Now the Fruit Earth—from which all life has arisen—is connected with everything that is alive. The Fire Earth is connected with everything that has sentience, with everything that experiences pleasure and pain and with the lower aspects of the soul, its passions and urges.

I can only give you a few glimpses of this vast area, to show how events upon the earth are connected to disturbances in the Fire and Fruit Earths. When the human being of today was first fructified with a higher soul principle and began to be human, tremendous drives were still active under the influence of the Fruit and Fire Earths. Everything was in a fury, raging in a way totally different from anything possible today. Human beings in Lemuria[2] were tremendously active. The whole Lemurian continent which lay between today's Australia, Asia and South Africa, perished in catastrophic volcanic eruptions brought about by the wild fury of the Fruit and Fire Earths. This was connected with human beings who at that time still lived entirely in their drives and instincts. A close connection existed then between drives, desires and passions on the one hand and volcanic activity on the other. The end of the Lemurian continent was brought about by the magnificent egotism of the last Lemurian races who practiced a form of black magic which is beyond our powers of imagination.

In the same way the destruction of Atlantis,[3] known as the

Flood, was connected with the moral quality of the Atlantean peoples. Only traces of this remain. Nevertheless, up to a certain point we can show a definite connection between the lives people led and such phenomena. We must, of course, be extremely cautious in establishing this, for it is only too easy for fantasies to creep in. One has to base oneself solely on facts determined by occult research. Occultists try to establish what happened when Vesuvius erupted in AD 79, when the earthquake happened in Calabria, when the earthquake took place at the time of Christ, or at the Lisbon earthquake of 1755. Many people died in those disasters. That people perished in them does not necessarily mean they did something in a previous life to deserve it. It is part of their karma that they should die in this manner. This is one reason why one looks at the karma of those who died this way. The other is the following. Theosophical handbooks often describe kamaloka and devachan as if they are merely a consequence, an after-effect, of the previous earth life. But actually the dead still work upon and influence earthly life. They play a role when changes occur on earth, in the phenomena of civilizations and in nature. Imagine for a moment that we were once born in the early years of Christianity and have been reborn in the present age. The fauna and flora of Europe would have changed tremendously in the meantime. Many animals and plant species would have become extinct, with others taking their place. The spiritual-scientific explanation of this is not something supernatural. The powers a person has when he is not in his body actually join forces with the forces of nature, so that human beings influence their future lives with the powers they possess in devachan or in kamaloka. If you see animals today that differ from those seen thousands of years ago, this is partially due to human influences. Human beings play a certain role in the forces of nature. The dead are continually involved in working on natural phenomena. In many respects we can regard events in nature as something which the dead bring about in *this* world.

The matter is not as simple with volcanic eruptions and earthquakes; nevertheless, these have something to do with human beings who have not yet reincarnated. They are definitely connected with the souls that incarnate when such earthquakes take place. As an occultist one has two questions to answer. First, what happens with the people who die in earthquakes? Second, what kind of people are born during an earthquake—so that they come down into this visible, perceptible world during such a time? Both investigations show a link between the disasters and the moral and intellectual qualities observed in humanity. It turns out that the people who perish in such tragic events are, quite apart from all their usual karmic tendencies, brought together with other souls in the spot where an earthquake occurs because of karmic realities. All the souls who die in such quakes are given the opportunity to overcome a final element that still blocks their karma, so that they may change from materialists into idealists and gain insight into spiritual matters.

On the other hand people who are born in such situations are, strangely enough, souls who have a definite attraction to drives, instincts and passions, and are born to be real materialists. People born under such influences become materialists, and generally speaking, practical materialists, people who are materialistic in their morality. The powers of nature are connected with the powers which human beings develop as their own in devachan. The forces which arise when the Fire Earth and Fruit Earth react in such disasters have an inner connection with souls who are destined to have an attitude of practical materialism in their next life. Souls born under the auspices of volcanic eruptions are truly materialistic unbelievers, people who want to know nothing of a life in the spirit.

We can state these two facts with certainty and you can easily see how things will continue to go in this direction in earth evolution. The more that human beings overcome genuine materialism, the fewer such disasters will there be on our earth. This force of attraction exists between materialism and what is found in the Fire and Fruit Earths. Our earth will grow calmer and more harmonious to the same extent that humanity becomes free of materialism.

A curious development has taken place with regard to materialism in recent centuries. As you know, I have always stressed that medieval times were more spiritual than our own age. The majority of people, at least in Europe, had more of a feeling for spirituality. Recent times have brought numerous volcanic eruptions, when materialism has been on the increase. Vesuvius is the only volcano still active on the mainland of Europe. Consider the number of its eruptions, with particularly severe ones recorded in AD 79, 203, 472, 512, 652, 982, 1036, 1139 ... 1872, 1885, 1891 ... 1906.

These figures may be read in any way that you want. All I can say is that occult teachings were popularized for much deeper reasons than people generally believe. Those who introduced them knew full well what should happen, namely, an intensive spiritual development of humanity in harmony with the great cosmic scheme of things. A lay person may show little interest in decisions made in the spiritual-scientific movement—the great, all-encompassing ideas about what happens not only about the human race but also the world. It may appear that we are concerned here with a set of teachings, a doctrine, but in reality we are concerned with something of tremendous depth and significance for the whole cosmos.

We have to emphasize these things again and again, so let me repeat myself. I have tried on this occasion to speak of something which is not normally mentioned, not even in our theosophical movement, presenting it to those who are accustomed to receive spiritual things in the right way. I have tried to refer to certain points which are connected with the most profound secrets of occultism. They can help you gain moral insight into the events we have experienced in the last few days. One thing, however, must be kept in mind. Beware of attaching anything fantastic to these complex and comprehensive situations. We must limit ourselves to what is substantiated by sound methods which have proved their value not just for thousands of years, but from the very beginnings of occultism. We should consider only those things which truly have their origin in initiation science, where access to these secrets is possible.

# The Interior of the Earth

21 April 1906

In light of the powerful events of nature we have heard of—
the eruption of Vesuvius and the earthquake in America—it
is quite obvious that students of spiritual science should ask if
there is any connection between the process of cosmic evolution on the one hand and human karma on the other. It is
enormously interesting to investigate and explain these
recent events from the occult point of view. In order to do so,
the occultist must not only be schooled in clairvoyance in the
usual way, but must have gone through an initiation in the
second degree. It is a known fact in occult circles that the
interior of the earth does not reveal itself to ordinary clairvoyance. It is relatively easy to have clairvoyant awareness at
the astral and devachanic planes. It requires another kind of
initiation to be able to explore the interior of the earth.

First of all let me remind you that present-day humanity
has only managed to penetrate the outer shell of the earth to a
very small depth. It has scarcely gone beyond 2,000 metres.
Everything else lies beyond its knowledge. People would
really be surprised, perhaps even confused, if they succeeded
in learning more about the deeper layers of our earth. They
would be confused because they would find things that show
only the faintest similarity to what we know upon the earth's
surface. They would have no words to describe most of them,
for the states of matter inside the earth are utterly different
from anything we know up here. They would be completely
amazed to find that the metal which corresponds to our silver

here is liquid down there, as mercury is liquid up here. The same holds true for the other metals and the minerals too.

The earth consists of seven distinct layers. An investigation of those seven layers corresponds to the seven stages of Christian initiation, which are:

1. The Washing of the Feet;
2. the Scourging;
3. the Crowning with Thorns;
4. the Crucifixion;
5. the Mystic Death on the Cross;
6. the Entombment;
7. the Resurrection.

Whoever has passed the first stage of initiation is able to penetrate the outermost layer clairvoyantly and proceed to explore the second layer, and so on.

In the first place, then, the earth has seven layers. The outermost layer where we live is called the Mineral Earth in the language of initiates. This and the other terms I will use come from a great occult school. These same terms were used by medieval mystics, Rosicrucians and others.

The Mineral Earth contains all the minerals with which we are familiar. It is an extremely thin and delicate layer, relatively speaking. Volcanic eruptions prove that deeper layers are able to penetrate it.

The Mineral Earth is followed by what is known as the Soft Earth. It is given that name because the hardening process has not gone as far there as it has in the Mineral Earth. It has a quite remarkable property, a kind of sentience. If touched it produces sentient responses similar to the dim conscious awareness of some plant species.

The next layer is called the Steam Earth. Just as steam is

produced in a boiler, so this layer displays a kind of will-like expression and is capable of enormous expansion. The mineral layer is able to contain it only with considerable effort.

The fourth layer is called the Form Earth, or the Water Earth. Its special feature is that it possesses the negative of every form we know of in the mineral layer. Thus, a rock crystal there would have the form of its negative, like a plaster cast up here.

The fifth layer is known as the Fruit Earth. If a portion of the Fruit Earth were able to get out into the atmosphere, we would observe form upon form arising from it and disappearing again. It has soul, as it were, the capacities of a soul struggling to gain shape and form.

The sixth layer is the Fire Earth—a most remarkable layer, as we shall see. It is able to feel pleasure and pain, so to speak, and is more or less like a human being who is 'sky high' one moment and 'down in the dumps' the next. Human passions have a tremendous effect upon the Fire Earth. The more human passions increase, the more restless it becomes.

The seventh layer is called the Earth Mirror precisely because everything that happens on the outermost layer is reflected here, although you must think of it happening in a different way. Everything passive here is active there, and vice versa. If you strike something metal here to make it ring, the metal rings of its own accord down there.

These seven layers are followed by two others of a very peculiar nature. In the School of Pythagoras the eighth layer was called the Sphere of Numbers because of a particular characteristic which we will consider in a moment. Our occult schools call it the Shatterer or Splinterer. If we were to hold a flower against it, trying to look at this layer through the flower, we would see a rose multiplied an infinite number of times. If we did the same experiment with a stone, no multiplication would take place. Multiplication only applies to natural life forms and to things created with artistic feeling. This region is the seat of all disharmony, immorality and unrest. Everything there strives against the other; it is the opposite of love. If a black magician were to succeed in reaching it—and he does have the power to do so—the evil in him would grow tremendously more powerful. The moral attitude of human beings has an enormous influence upon this layer. If humanity succeeds in progressively ridding itself of immorality, replacing it with morality, this zone will gradually calm down. This will, in turn, influence the attitudes of human beings.

The ninth and final layer is the dwelling place of the spirit of our planet and has two peculiar features. One may compare it with a human being, for it has an organ resembling a brain. Another organ is similar to a heart. Also, the planetary spirit is subject to changes which are closely connected with human evolution.

Now let us return to the Fire Earth. As noted earlier, it displays the capacity to feel pleasure and pain. People's passions have a powerful influence on it, so that it gets into an even greater state of disturbance and upheaval when human beings develop great passions. Then it exerts even greater pressure on the Fruit Earth which lies above it. Channels branch out from the Fire Earth to all of the layers above it. The Mineral Earth contains great cavities or hollows, although these lie at considerable depths. Channels run from the Fruit Earth to those hollow spaces and force tremendous amounts of material into them which, for their part, either cause earthquakes or seek a way out through the vents of a volcano. Recent disasters were caused in this fashion.

The third great root race, the Lemurians, still lived on the Soft Earth. The hardening process of the outer crust had not progressed very far and there were just a few harder areas which floated in this soft layer more or less like islands. The last remnants and evidence of the Soft Earth are the many small islands in the Pacific which rise suddenly above the surface of the ocean and disappear again after a time. The Lemurians, who developed tremendous passions, so influenced the Fire Earth as their evolution progressed and they indulged in their vices, that the Fire Earth grew rebellious, so to speak, rose up to the surface with tremendous power and destroyed the race. Thus we see that the Lemurians brought about their own destruction. Realizing this, the occultist reflects that by working on his own perfection he may not only accelerate the process of evolution for his own time, but may also have considerable influence upon earth evolution. This should arouse a feeling of responsibility in both directions, spurring him to do further work upon himself.

Let us now consider two highly important occult facts which are connected with these events in nature. On the one hand let us envision the karma of people who have perished in such disasters. It is only natural for people to wonder about the enormous karma falling upon countless individuals on such occasions. I can tell you, however, that occult observation has shown that these souls become very spiritual in their next incarnation. Their violent death came as the final shock which stripped off the bonds of materialism once and for all.

Another observation from occultism is that all the people born when such volcanic eruptions take place will become

materialists during their lifetime. This is quite understandable. The disturbing element of the Fire Earth influences them while they are trying with all their strength to
reincarnate, and gives them materialistic qualities. It is all the
same whether a soul is born here or in America, for example;
spacial separation has no effect in this realm. Many readers
and writers of materialistic works were born around the year
1822, when Vesuvius erupted after a long period of quies-
cence. The fact that Vesuvius remained dormant for centuries[1] is a reflection of the spiritual character of the Middle
Ages. Since then eruptions have come at relatively short
intervals. Evolution has speeded up altogether now. The
period from Charlemagne[2] to Frederick the Great[3,4] corresponds to the nineteenth century. That is to say: all the events
during the longer period correspond in number and significance to what happens now within a single century.
Evolution will proceed even faster as time goes on.

# Earthquakes, Volcanoes and the Human Will (excerpt)

12 June 1906

Physical science as yet knows only of the terrestrial crust, a mineral layer which is merely a thin skin at the surface of the earth. In reality the earth consists of a succession of concentric layers which we shall now describe.

1. The mineral layer contains all the metals found in the physical bodies of everything that lives at the surface. This crust, formed like a skin around the living being of the earth, is only a few miles deep.

2. The second layer can only be understood if we envisage a substance which is the very opposite of what we know. It is negative life, the opposite of life. All life is extinguished there. If a plant or animal were plunged into it, it would be destroyed immediately and be totally dissolved. This second shell—half liquid—which envelops the earth is truly a realm of death.

3. The third layer is a realm of inverted consciousness. All sorrow appears there as joy, and every joy is experienced as sorrow. It is composed of vapours and is related to our feelings in the same negative manner as the second layer is related to life. If we now conceptualize these three layers we would find the earth in the condition it was in before the separation of the Old Moon. If, through concentration, one attains conscious astral vision, one would see the activities in these two layers: the destruction of life in the second layer, and the transformation and inversion of feelings in the third.

4. The fourth layer, known as Water Earth, Soul Earth, or Form Earth, is endowed with a remarkable property. Let us imagine a cube. Now picture it reversed inasmuch as its substance is concerned. Where once there was substance, now there is nothing. The space occupied by the cube is now empty, while its substance, or substantial form, is spread around it—hence the term Form Earth. This whirlwind of forms, instead of being a negative emptiness, becomes a positive substance.

5. This layer is called the earth of expansive growth. It contains the archetypal source of all terrestrial life, and its substance consists of burgeoning, teeming energies.

6. The sixth layer is the Fire Earth, which is composed of pure will, of elemental life-forces in constant movement permeated with drives and passions—a veritable reservoir of will forces. If you exert pressure on this substance it offers opposition and fights back. If we conceptualize these last three layers, we arrive at the condition of our globe when Sun, Moon and Earth were still interwoven as a single body.

The following layers are only accessible to a conscious awareness maintained not just in dreamless sleep, but in deep sleep.

7. This layer is the Mirror Earth. It is like a prism which decomposes everything reflected in it and brings to expression its polaric counterpart. An emerald would appear as red if viewed through the Mirror Earth.

8. Everything appears in this layer as fragmented and reproduced to infinity. If we take a plant or a crystal and concentrate on this layer, the plant or crystal appears indefinitely multiplied.

9. This last layer is composed of a substance endowed with moral action, but a morality which is the opposite of what

must be developed on earth. Its essence, its inherent force, is separation, discord and hate. Here in the hell of Dante, we find Cain the fratricide. This substance is the opposite of everything good and beautiful among men. Human activities which promote brotherhood on earth weaken the power of this sphere. The power of love will transform this layer, inasmuch as it will spiritualize the very body of the earth. This ninth layer is the substantive source of what appears on earth as black magic, that is, a magic founded upon egotism.

These various layers are connected by rays which link the centre of the earth with its surface. In the outer layer, but in the bowels of the solid earth, are a large number of subterranean cavities which are linked to the sixth layer, the Fire Earth. The Fire Earth is intimately connected with the human will. The Fire Earth produced the tremendous eruptions that brought the Lemurian epoch to an end. At that time the forces which feed the human will went through a trial which unleashed the fire catastrophe that destroyed the Lemurian continent. In the course of evolution this sixth layer has receded more and more toward the centre of the earth and, as a result, volcanic eruptions have become less frequent. And yet they are still caused by the will of human beings which, when it is evil and chaotic, magnetically acts upon this layer and disrupts it. Nevertheless, when the human will is free from egotism, it is able to appease this fire. Materialistic periods in particular are accompanied and followed by natural catastrophes, earthquakes, and so forth. A stronger adherence to the progressive powers of evolution is the only alchemy which can transform, little by little, the organism and soul of the earth.

The following offers an example of the relationship which exists between the human will and movements of the earth.

One can observe in people who have died in earthquakes or volcanic eruptions that their inner qualities are quite different in their next incarnation. They bring with them a great predisposition to spiritual matters at birth because, through their death, they were brought in touch with forces which showed them the true nature of reality and the illusion of material life.

One has also noticed a relationship between certain births and seismic and volcanic catastrophes. Materialistic souls incarnate during such catastrophes, drawn sympathetically by volcanic phenomena and by the convulsions of the evil soul of the earth. These births can, in turn, bring about new cataclysms because the evil souls exert a reciprocal, stimulating influence upon the chthonic fire. The evolution of our planet is intimately connected with the evolution of the forces of humanity and its civilizations.

# Rosicrucian Training, The Interior of the Earth, Earthquakes and Volcanoes (excerpt)

4 September 1906

We have gone into the various methods of [Rosicrucian] training. I will end these lectures by showing you something about the relationship between the human being and the whole earth, so that you will see how the human being is connected to everything that happens on the earth.

I have described human evolution and shown how it can develop itself ever higher. In the course of evolution the whole of humanity will attain everything an individual can achieve through occult training. But what will happen to the earth while mankind is developing this way? There is a great difference between the earth as seen by the occultist and the earth known to the ordinary geologist or scientist. He looks on it as merely a sort of great lifeless ball, with an interior not very unlike its exterior, except that at most the interior substances are fluid. But it is not easy to understand how such a lifeless ball could have produced all the different kinds of beings on it.

We know that various phenomena occur on earth which deeply affect the fate of many people; yet, present-day science looks on this as a purely external relationship. The fate of hundreds and thousands of people may be affected by an earthquake or a volcano. Does the human will influence these things, or is it all a matter of chance? Do dead, natural laws act with blind fury, or does some connection exist between these events and the human will? What really happens when a person is killed by an earthquake? What does the occultist say about the interior of the earth?

The occult science of every epoch states that the earth consists of a series of layers not totally separated from one another, like the skins of an onion, but which gradually merge into one another.

1. The topmost layer, the mineral mass, is related to the interior as an eggshell is related to an egg. This topmost layer is called the Mineral Earth.

2. Beneath it is a second layer called the Fluid Earth which consists of substances comparable to nothing upon the earth. It is unlike any fluid we are familiar with, for these all have a mineral quality. This layer has special characteristics and displays certain spiritual qualities, since as soon as it is brought into contact with something living, it tries to expel and destroy that life. An occultist is able to investigate this layer by pure concentration.

3. The Air Earth is a substance which destroys sensations. For instance, if it is brought into contact with any pain, the pain is converted into pleasure, and vice versa. The original quality of the sensation is extinguished, just as the second layer extinguishes life.

4. The Water Earth or Form Earth. This layer consists of forces which produce effects in the material realm which occur spiritually in devachan. The negative images of physical things are found here. For example, in the Form Earth a cube of salt would be destroyed, but its negative would arise. The form is, as it were, changed into its opposite; all of its qualities pass out into its surroundings. The actual space occupied by the object is left empty.

5. The Fruit Earth is a substance which is full of exuberant energy. Every bit of it grows out at once like sponge; it

grows larger and larger and is held in place only by the upper layers. It is the underlying life which serves the layers above it.

6. The Fire Earth is made essentially of feeling and will. It is sensitive to pain and would cry out if stepped on. It consists entirely of passions.

7. The Earth Mirror or Reflector Earth. This layer gets its name from the fact that, if one concentrates on it, it changes all the characteristics of the earth into their opposites. If the seer disregards everything lying above it and gazes directly down into this layer, and if he then, for example, places something green before him, the green appears as red. Every colour appears as its complementary opposite. A polaric reflection arises, a reversal of the original. Sorrow is changed into joy by this substance.

8. The Splintering Earth. If one concentrates on it with developed power something very remarkable appears. For example, a plant held in the midst of this layer appears as if multiplied, and so does everything else. The essential thing is that this layer shatters moral qualities as well. Through the power it radiates up to the earth's surface, it is responsible for the fact that strife and disharmony exist. Human beings must work together in harmony in order to overcome this disruptive force.

That is precisely why this layer was laid down into the earth—so that human beings have to develop harmony for themselves. Everything evil is essentially prepared and organized here. Quarrelsome people are so constituted that this layer has a special influence on them. This has been known to everyone who has written out of a true knowledge of occultism. Dante[1] calls this the Cain-layer in *The Divine Comedy*. The strife between the brothers Cain and Abel had

its source here. This layer is responsible for having brought
evil into the world.

9. The Earth Core is the substance through whose influence black magic arises in the world. The power of spiritual
evil comes from this source.

You can see from the above that human beings are related
to all of these layers, for they continually radiate out their
forces. Humanity lives under the influence of these layers and
has to overcome their energies. One day, when human beings
have learned to radiate life and have trained their breathing
so that it promotes life, they will overcome the Fire Earth.
When spiritually they overcome pain through serenity, they
will overcome the Air Earth. When peace and harmony reign,
the Splintering Earth will be conquered. When white magic
triumphs, no more evil will remain on the earth. Thus,
human evolution implies a transformation of the earth's
interior. In the beginning the nature of the earth's body was
such as to hold subsequent developments in check. In the
end, when human powers have transformed the earth, the
earth will be spiritualized. In this way human beings impart
their own being to the earth.

There are times when the passions in the Fire Earth rebel.
Aroused by human passions, the Fire Earth penetrates
through the Fruit Earth, forces its way through the channels
in the upper layers, flows up into and violently shakes the
solid earth. The result is an earthquake. A volcano erupts
when passions from the Fire Earth thrust up some of the
earth's substance. All of this is closely connected with
humanity. In Lemurian times the upper layer was still very
soft and the Fire Earth was close to the surface. Human
passions and the passion-substance of this layer are related.
When people give rein to evil passions they strengthen its

passions; that is what happened at the end of Lemurian times. The Lemurians made the Fire Earth rebellious through their passions, and in this way brought about the destruction of the entire Lemurian continent. No other cause for this destruction could be found except in what they themselves had drawn forth from the earth. Today the layers are thicker and firmer, but there still exists this connection between human passions and the Passion Layer in the interior of the earth. The accumulation of evil passions and energies still gives rise to earthquakes and volcanic eruptions.

The way in which a person's destiny and will are connected to occurrences in the earth can be seen from two examples which have been fully investigated occultly. It has been found that people who have been killed in an earthquake appear in their next incarnation as individuals of high spiritual quality and faith. They had progressed far enough to be convinced, by that final stroke, of the transitoriness of earthly matters. The effect of this in devachan was that they learned a lesson for their next life: that matter is perishable, but the spirit prevails. All of them did not come to this realization, but many are alive today as people who belong to some spiritual-theosophical movement.

In the other example, people were investigated whose births coincided with an earthquake or a volcanic eruption. It was found that all these people were, strangely enough, persons of a very materialistic cast of mind. The earthquakes and volcanic eruptions did not cause this; rather, those strongly materialistic souls, ripe for birth, worked their way down into the physical world through their astral will and let loose the forces of the Fire Earth, which caused tremors at the time they were born.

So the will of human beings is connected with what happens on earth. One transforms one's dwelling place and one's self at the same time. When a person spiritualizes himself, he spiritualizes the earth as well. One day, at a later planetary stage, he will have ennobled the earth through his own creative power. In every moment that we think and feel, we are working on the great edifice of the earth. The leaders of humanity have insight into such relationships and try to give human beings forces which work in the true direction of evolution.

# Mephistopheles and Earthquakes

1 January 1909

The theme of today's lecture has a profoundly occult character. The title, strange as it may seem to begin with, is 'Mephistopheles and Earthquakes'. We will see that not only does the figure of Mephistopheles lead us into a deep realm of occultism, but that the same applies to the problem of earthquakes, if discussed from the spiritual point of view. I have already spoken here and in several other places about the interior of the earth and have also referred to the question of earthquakes. We will now approach the subject of these extraordinarily tragic events on the earth's surface from yet another side.

The figure of Mephistopheles, our starting point today, is familiar to all of you from Goethe's *Faust*. You know that Mephistopheles is a being. We shall not enter today into the question of how far the poetic presentation tallies with the occult facts. You know that this figure, who appears in the drama as the seducer and tempter of Faust, in a certain respect represents someone who aspires to reach the heights of existence. In lectures on Goethe I have indicated what spiritual vistas are revealed in the scene of the 'Passage to the Mothers', where Mephistopheles holds in his hand the key giving access to the dark, subterranean regions where the Mothers dwell.[1] Mephistopheles himself is unable to enter this region. He merely points out that in this region there is no difference between 'below' and 'above':

'Sink then! I might as well say, Mount up!'[2]

Both mean the same thing in this mysterious realm. We know too, that in characterizing this region, Mephistopheles uses the word 'naught', or 'nothingness' ['Nichts' in German]. In a certain sense he represents the spirit who perceives something valueless in this 'nothingness'. Faust answers as any true seeker today might reply to a materialistic thinker: 'In your Nothingness I hope to find the All'.[3]

Goethean research has made many attempts to find the clue to the figure of Mephistopheles. In other lectures I have said that the explanation of the name Mephistopheles is found in the Hebrew language, where 'Mephiz' is the word for one who obstructs, who corrupts, and 'tophel' for one who lies. Thus, we must think of this name as belonging to a being who brings corruption and hindrances to human beings and is a spirit of untruth, deception and illusion.

It may occur to thoughtful readers of the Introduction to *Faust*, the 'Prologue in Heaven', that it contains words which resound across thousands of years. Goethe let words be spoken at the beginning of *Faust* which echo the words spoken between the Lord and Job in the Book of Job.[4] You only have to read in the Book of Job about how Job is a good, upright and pious man and of how the Sons of the Lord of Light present themselves before God. Among them is a certain Enemy of the Light. In a conversation between the Enemy of the Light and the Supreme Lord, the Enemy of the Light says that he has 'gone to and fro upon the earth', seeking and trying out many things. The Lord asks: 'Do you know my servant Job?' And the Enemy of the Light (for so we will call him) answers that he knows him and that he would certainly be able to turn Job away from the path of goodness and bring him to perdition. You know that this spirit has to make two attempts to approach Job and that he lays hold of Job by injuring his outer, physical body. He indicates this clearly when he says to the Lord: 'If you seize his possessions, he will not fall; but if you catch hold of his bone and his flesh, then he will fall!' Who can fail to hear an echo of this in *Faust* when the Lord calls to Mephistopheles in the 'Prologue in Heaven': 'Do you know my servant Faust?' Then, in similar terms, we hear the retort of the spirit who in the Book of Job comes before the Lord, when Mephistopheles asserts that he can lead Faust gently on the way, saying that he can lead him away from the paths which lead to the Good. We are listening here to words which resound across the ages.

If you think about Mephistopheles, you may have often asked yourselves: who is Mephistopheles really? Grave mistakes are made here, mistakes which admittedly can only be corrected by a deeper, occult insight. The name itself suggests that Mephistopheles is associated with the devil, or the idea of the devil, for the word 'tophel' is the same as *Teufel*—devil. But the other question—and here we enter a realm of serious fallacies which frequently occur in explanations about Mephistopheles—the other question is: can Mephistopheles be identified with the spirit we know as Lucifer who, together with his hosts, approached mankind during and after the Lemurian epoch and entrenched himself within human evolution? The prevailing tendency in Europe is to identify Mephistopheles, as he appears in Goethe's *Faust* and also in earlier folk-literature (folk-plays, puppet-plays and so forth), with Lucifer. Mephistopheles is a familiar character everywhere, and the question is: are he and his hosts identical with Lucifer and his hosts? In other words: are the effects of the Mephistophelian influence upon humanity the same as those of Lucifer? That is the question before us today.

We know when Lucifer approached humanity. We have studied the course of human evolution on earth through the epoch when the sun and later the moon separated from the earth together with those forces which would have made further development impossible for human beings. We have seen that Lucifer and his hosts approached mankind at a time when the human being was still not ready for his astral body to become independent. The effect upon mankind was twofold. Man's astral body was exposed to the influences issuing from Lucifer towards the end of the Lemurian epoch. If Lucifer had not intervened, humanity, it is true, would have been protected from certain evils; but it would not have attained what must be accounted as one of its greatest blessings.

The significance of Lucifer's influence becomes evident when we ask ourselves: what would have happened if, from the Lemurian epoch on, there had been no Luciferic influence, if Lucifer and his hosts had remained separate and apart from human evolution? Man would have evolved until the middle of the Atlantean epoch as a being who, in every impulse of his astral body, would have obeyed the influences of certain spiritual beings ranked higher than himself. These beings would have dominated him until the middle of the Atlantean epoch. If that had happened, mankind's faculties of perception and cognition would not have been directed towards the material world until a much later date. During the Lemurian and early Atlantean epochs no passions or desires would have arisen from their sense perception. Human beings would have confronted the sense world in a state of innocence, obedient in every action to the impulses instilled into them by higher spiritual beings. The instincts motivating them would not have been precisely the same as those motivating the higher animals today, but would have been more spiritual. Their every deed on earth would have been prompted by a kind of spiritual instinct and not by mere sensual impulses. As things were, under Lucifer's influence man arrived earlier at the stage where he said: this makes me happy, this attracts me, that repels me! He reached the stage of following his own impulses earlier than would otherwise have been the case. He became an independent being enjoying a certain degree of freedom. The consequence was that he was, in a certain respect, detached from the spiritual world.

To put it concisely, one may say: without Lucifer's influence, the human being would have remained a spiritualized animal, an animal who would have gradually developed a form nobler and more beautiful than could have been developed under Lucifer's influence. Man would have remained far more of an angelic being if Lucifer's influence had not entered into him in the Lemurian epoch. But on the other hand, higher beings would have guided him, so to speak, on leading-strings. In the middle of the Atlantean epoch something would suddenly have happened to him. His eyes would have been fully opened and the tapestry of the whole sense world would have lain around him. But, when gazing upon it, he would have perceived the divine-spiritual at the same time, a world with a divine-spiritual foundation lying behind every physical object. If, in his former state of dependence, man had looked back into the bosom of the Divine where he had come from, beholding the Gods of Light sending their radiance into his soul, guiding and leading him, the effect would have been—this is not merely a picture, but corresponds to a high degree with reality—that the entire sense world would have been transparent before him, revealing those other divine-spiritual beings behind it who had taken the place of what had been lost. One spiritual world would have closed behind him and a new spiritual world would have opened in front of him. Man would have remained a child in the hands of higher, divine-spiritual beings. The capacity for independence would not have been established in his soul.

It did not happen this way because Lucifer had set to work on man and made part of the underlying spiritual world invisible to him. The personal instincts, passions and desires which rose up in the human astral body spread a cloud of darkness over the spiritual beings from the world of man's origin and who otherwise would have always remained visible to him.

Hence in those great centres, the Oracles of ancient Atlantis, the initiates had expressly trained themselves to see into that part of the spiritual world which had been hidden by Lucifer's influence. The aim of all the preparation undergone by the guardians and pupils of the ancient Oracles in the Atlantean Mysteries was to enable them to perceive that part of the spiritual world of light which, as a result of Lucifer's influence upon the human astral body, had withdrawn from man's field of vision. Also visible were those figures seen by man in the various conditions of soul running parallel with initiation, figures which penetrate into our world decked in astral raiment from a world of light. In the ancient Oracle centres the Atlantean initiate spiritually saw beings of a higher rank who had not descended into the physical world and who remained invisible to ordinary sight after humanity's eyes were prematurely opened. But, since Lucifer himself opposed these worlds of light, it was inevitable that he, too, should be visible to the initiates. The hosts of Lucifer *were* visible to the Atlanteans who with their shadowy, clairvoyant consciousness could be transported into the spiritual world while asleep and in the state of consciousness midway between sleeping and waking. When part of the world of light was accessible to these people, part of the opposing world was also visible. The Luciferic hosts were visible—not Lucifer himself. As fascinating and as splendid appeared these noble figures of the world of light in their spectrum of astral colour, so equally frightening and terrible appeared their opponents, who belonged to the world of temptation.

So we can say that Lucifer's influence upon human evolution made it possible for man to fall into error and evil, but it also made it possible for him to attain freedom. If there had been no Luciferic influence, the conditions I have been describing would have come about in the middle of the Atlantean epoch. The tapestry of the sense world would have been outspread before humanity. The mineral, plant and animal kingdoms would have been materially visible to him, as well as the phenomena of nature and of the heavens— thunder, lightning, clouds, air—all would have been visible to external sight. But behind it all would have been the unmistakable presence of divine-spiritual beings who would have pressed in upon humanity. Because Lucifer's influence had already affected man's astral body, his physical body—at that time still capable of transformation—had been prepared since the Lemurian epoch and on into the Atlantean so that it could not become the direct instrument for the physical sense world with the spiritual world standing visibly behind it. Man could not immediately behold the physical sense-world in a form which simultaneously revealed itself as a spiritual world. The three lower kingdoms of nature lay around him. The physical world in these circumstances became like a veil, a thick cover, over the spiritual world. Man could not, nor can he to this day, see directly into the spiritual world.

But because humanity passed through this evolution a different influence was able to assert itself in the middle of the Atlantean epoch, an influence from quite another side, one not to be confused with Lucifer and his hosts. Although Lucifer first made it possible for man to come under the sway of this other influence, although Lucifer caused the human physical body to become denser than it otherwise would have become, nevertheless it was necessary for yet another influence to approach man to bring him completely into the material sense-world, to shut him off completely from the spiritual world so that he was led to the illusion: there is no other world than the material existence spread out before me!

From the middle of the Atlantean epoch forward an opponent quite different in character from Lucifer approached man, namely, the being who casts such fog and darkness around man's faculties of perception that he makes no effort, nor unfolds any urge, to fathom the secrets of the sense world. If you picture to yourselves that under Lucifer's influence the sense world became like a veil, through the influence of this second being the entire physical world became like a dense rind closing off the spiritual world. Only the Atlantean initiates were able to pierce this dense blanket of the physical world through the preparations they had undergone.

The powers who approached man to obscure his vision of the other side of divine existence are first brought to our notice in the teachings which Zarathustra, the great leader of the ancient Persians, gave to his followers and pupils. The mission of Zarathustra was to instil culture into a people who, unlike the ancient Indians, did not by nature constantly yearn for the spiritual world. Zarathustra's mission was to impart to his people a culture directed to the sense world, aiming at mastery of the material world through the efforts and labours of physical man. Humanity was less subject to Lucifer's influence in ancient Persia than to the influence of that being who had approached mankind since the middle of the Atlantean epoch. The result was that many initiates at that time lapsed into the practice of a kind of black magic. Led astray by this tempter, they misused what was accessible to them from the spiritual world for the purposes of the physical-material world. The powerful influence of black magic which finally led to the destruction of Atlantis had its origin in the temptations of the being whom Zarathustra taught his people to know as Ahriman (Angra Mainyu), the being who opposed the God of Light proclaimed by Zarathustra as Ahura Mazdao, the 'Great Aura'.

These two figures, Lucifer and Ahriman, must be clearly distinguished from each other. Lucifer is a being who detached himself from the spiritual hosts of heaven *after* the separation of the sun. Ahriman had already broken away *before* the separation of the sun and is an embodiment of quite different powers. The result of Lucifer's influence in the Lemurian epoch was merely the corruption of the ability to manipulate the forces of air and water, an ability still possessed by Atlantean humanity. In the book *Cosmic Memory*[5] you have read that in Atlantean times the seminal forces in plants and animals were still at man's command and could be extracted, just as the forces of steam used for powering machines can be extracted from coal today. I told you that when these seed forces are drawn forth they are connected in a mysterious way with the nature-forces in wind, weather and the like. If man uses them for purposes running counter to the divine purposes, these nature-forces are called into action against him.

This is the cause of the Atlantean flood and of the devastation wrought by the nature forces which led to the sinking of the whole Atlantean continent. Even before that time human beings had lost command over the forces of fire and the power to ally them with certain mysterious forces of the earth. Power over the forces of fire and earth in a certain combination had already been withdrawn from man. But now, through the influence of Ahriman and his accomplices, man again acquired a certain mastery over the forces of fire and earth with dire consequences. Much that is heard about the use of fire in ancient Persia is connected with what I am telling you now. Many forces employed in black magic and connected with it lead to the result that man lays hold of forces of an entirely different nature and thereby gains influence over fire and earth, with terrible and devastating results. The practice of black magic by the Atlantean descendants in ancient Persia would have been effective had not the teachings of Zarathustra revealed how Ahriman, as an opposing power, ensnares man and clouds his vision of the spiritual reality behind the sense world. So, we see that through Zarathustra and his adherents influence was brought to bear upon a large part of post-Atlantean civilization. On the one hand people were taught about the activity of the sublime God of Light who they may turn to, and on the other, they were taught about the pernicious power of Ahriman and his hosts.

Ahriman works upon man through diverse ways and

means. I have told you that the Event of Golgotha[6] was a moment of supreme importance for world evolution. Christ appeared in the realm man enters after death, where Ahriman's influence was much stronger than in the world around man between birth and death. Ahriman's influence worked upon man with terrible power and strength especially in the world between death and rebirth. If nothing else had happened, utter darkness would gradually have closed in upon man in the 'Realm of Shades'—as it was appropriately called by the ancient Greeks. A condition of complete isolation would have set in between death and rebirth, leading to the intensification of egotism. Man would have been born into his new life as a gross and overbearing egotist. It is more than a figure of speech to say that after the Event of Golgotha, at the moment when the blood flowed from His wounds, Christ appeared in the 'Realm of Shades' and cast Ahriman into chains. Although Ahriman's influence remains and is really the origin of all materialistic thinking on humanity's part, this influence can be paralyzed only if people receive into themselves the power emanating from the Mystery of Golgotha. They can draw from that event a strength which enables them to find their way once again into the divine-spiritual world.

Thus, Ahriman's activity was primarily directed at the faculty of human cognition. Man divined the existence of Ahriman, a being whom they had some knowledge of through the culture inaugurated by Zarathustra. From there knowledge of Ahriman spread among other peoples and into their world of ideas. Ahriman with his hosts appears among civilized peoples with the most diverse names. Owing to the peculiar conditions in the souls of the European peoples, who had remained farthest behind in the migrations from West to East[7] and who had been less affected than others by what occurred in the ancient Indian, Persian, Egyptian and Greco-Latin civilizations, owing to these circumstances there prevailed among the European peoples, from whom the Fifth Cultural Epoch was to be born, an attitude of soul which regarded Ahriman as a figure of dread. And while various names for Ahriman were adopted—among the Hebrew people he was called 'Mephistopheles'—in Europe he became the figure of the 'Devil' in various guises.

Obviously we are gazing here into deep connections within the spiritual worlds. Many people who claim to be above medieval superstitions will do well to remember the aphorism found in *Faust:*

'The little folk ne'er scent the Devil
E'en though he have them by the collar'.[8]

It is precisely because a person closes his spiritual eyes to this influence that he succumbs to it so completely. Goethe's 'Mephistopheles' is none other than Ahriman and we should not confuse him with Lucifer. All the errors cropping up here and there in commentaries on *Faust* originate from this confusion, although Lucifer first made Ahriman's influence possible. In studying Ahriman one is led back to the original influence of Lucifer, which only becomes clear after long preparations have been made to understand this intimate connection.

The subtle difference between these two beings must not be overlooked. The essential point is that Lucifer brought man under the influence of the powers connected with air and water *only;* whereas Ahriman-Mephistopheles has subjected him to the influence of far more dreadful powers. The civilizations immediately following ours will see the appearance of many things connected with Ahriman's influence.

Through this influence the spiritual seeker who does not stand upon firm and sure foundations can easily fall prey to the most terrible illusion and deception. For Ahriman is a spirit who sets out to spread deception as to the true nature of the sense world, especially as it is an expression of the spiritual world. When a person has a tendency to abnormal, somnambulistic states or through certain wrongful training awakens occult forces which intensify egotism, Ahriman-Mephistopheles has a ready influence precisely upon these occult forces, an influence which can easily grow more powerful. Whereas Lucifer's influence only causes what confronts man from the spiritual world to appear as an *astral* form visible to the astral body (and this applies also to one receiving improper training), the phenomena caused by Ahriman's influence are brought to light by evil influences which press upon, then press through, the physical body into the etheric body, where they then become visible *as phantoms*.

With Ahriman's influences we have to do with much, much lower forces than Lucifer's. Lucifer's influences can never become as bad as Ahriman's and of those beings connected with the powers of fire. Ahriman's influence can cause one to undertake certain practices with the physical body in order to attain occult knowledge. The method that consists in the use and misuse of the physical body is the most grievous that can possibly be employed in acquiring occult powers. It is a fact that in certain schools of black magic such practices are taught in abundance. Some of the most terrible seductions of human nature occur when the forces of the physical body are taken as the starting point for occult training.

It is not possible here to enter into greater detail than to indicate that all machinations consisting in any way of a misuse of the forces of the physical body emanate from the influence of Ahriman. Because their effects penetrate into man's etheric body, it works as a world of phantoms that is nothing other than the garment of powers which drag man down to a level below his true manhood. Nearly every ancient civilization—the Indian, Persian, Egyptian, the Greco-Latin—had its period of decadence. So, too, had the Mysteries, when the mystery-traditions were no longer preserved in their purity. During these periods many people fell into perverse and evil paths who were either pupils of the initiates, but unable to remain at their level, or people to whom the secrets of the Mysteries had been unlawfully betrayed. Centres of black magic originated from these influences and have continued to exist to the present time.

Ahriman, working with his followers in the spiritual world, is a spirit of lies, a spirit who conjures illusions before men. Ahriman himself is no mirage—far from it! But what is conjured before human spiritual vision under his influence, *that* is a mirage, an illusion. When a person's desires and passions flow along evil paths and at the same time he lends himself in any way to occult practices, then the occult forces which are awakened penetrate into the etheric body. The most evil powers of corruption then appear among the illusory images, which may often be majestic and awe-inspiring. Such is Ahriman's terrible influence upon human beings.

From what has been said you can gather that through Christ's Coming Ahriman has been cast into chains—if this expression may be used—but only for those who try ever and again to fathom the Christ-Mystery. Protection against Ahriman's influence in the world will steadily diminish except for the forces streaming from the Christ-Mystery. In a certain sense, and many signs proclaim it, our epoch courts Ahrimanic influences. In certain occult teachings Ahriman's hosts are also called the *Asuras*. These are the evil Asuras who at a certain time fell away from the evolutionary path of the Asuras who endowed man with personality.[9] It was indicated that these beings detached themselves from earth evolution *before* the separation of the sun.

Up to now we have described the terrible influence that Ahriman can exercise upon abnormal processes of development that proceed along occult paths. But in a certain respect the whole of humanity came under Ahriman's influence during the second half of the Atlantean epoch. The whole post-Atlantean epoch shows within it the aftermath of Ahriman's influence—in one region of the earth more, in another less. But Ahriman's influence has asserted itself everywhere. All the teachings given by the ancient initiates concerning the Spirits of Light, the opponents of Ahriman, were given primarily to pull people away from the influence of Ahriman. It was a well-prepared, well-led and wise education of humanity.

But let us not forget that since that time Ahriman's destiny has been interwoven with the destiny of humanity, and numerous occurrences, which the uninitiated know nothing about, keep the whole karma of humanity in a continuing connection with the karma of Ahriman. To understand this we must realize that a universal karmic law operates at every level of existence over and above the karma which belongs to every individual human being. All categories of beings have their karma—the karma of the one differing from that of the other. But karma operates through every realm of existence. There are things in the karma of humanity, in the karma of a people, of a community or other group, which must be regarded as collective karma, so that in certain circumstances an individual can be drawn into the sway of a collective karma. It is not always easy for one who is unable to penetrate to the root of the matter to discern exactly where the influences lie with persons who are overtaken by such a destiny. An individual within a given community may well be entirely guiltless, as far as his own karma is concerned. But, because he stands within a field of collective karma, some calamity may happen to him. However, if he is completely guiltless, compensation will be made in subsequent incarnations.

In a wider connection we must look not only at the karma of the past but also consider the karma of the future. We can quite correctly imagine that a terrible fate may befall an entire group of people. The reason why just this particular group should suffer such a destiny cannot be discovered. In certain circumstances someone capable of investigating an individual's karma will be unable to find anything that could have led to this tragic fate, for the threads of karma are extremely complicated. The cause of such karmic events may lie far, far away, but the cause is connected with these people nevertheless. It may be that the entire group, while guiltless, has been overtaken by some collective karma which could not strike those directly at fault, because circumstances made this impossible. In such cases the only thing to be said is this: everything is ultimately balanced out in the total karma of an individual, including what happens to him without any fault on his part. It is all inscribed in his karma. Compensation in the fullest sense will be made some time in the future. Therefore, in considering the law of karma we must also take into account the karmic future. We must not forget that each person is not just an isolated being but that every individual shares jointly in the collective karma of humanity. We must remember, too, that along with humanity, each person is connected with those hierarchies who have not entered into the physical world and that each person is also drawn into the karma of the hierarchies. Many things happen in human destiny in the physical world whose connections are not found in the immediate circumstances involving those things; but, their karmic consequences inevitably come to pass.

Since the second half of the Atlantean epoch Ahriman's karma has been linked with human karma. Where then, is Ahriman active, over and above what he fashions in human bodies to spread phantoms and illusion over the sense world? Where, then, are his other activities?

Everything in the world has two sides: one pertaining more to the human being as a spiritual being, the other to what has developed as the kingdoms of nature around him. The earth is the arena of human existence. The earth is revealed to the eye of spirit as a combination of different layers or strata. The outermost stratum is called the Mineral Earth, or Mineral Stratum, because it contains only the substances found in the ground under our feet. This is the shallowest stratum, relatively speaking. Then begins the Fluid Earth which consists of material entirely different from the Mineral Stratum above it. This second layer is endowed with inner life, and its forces are held together only because the solid, mineral layer is spread over it. If released, they would instantly disperse into cosmic space. This stratum, therefore, lies under tremendous pressure. A third layer is the Vapour Earth. It is not a material vapour such as arises on the earth's surface. In this third stratum the substance itself is imbued with inner forces, comparable only to the passions, the inner urges and impulses of the human being. Whereas on earth only animals and human beings unfold passions, this third stratum is permeated in a material sense with forces similar to human and animal passions and impulses, just as earthly substances are permeated by forces of magnetism and warmth. Then we have as the fourth stratum the Form Layer, so designated because it contains the material and forces encountered in the Mineral Earth as entities cast into form. The fifth layer, the Fruit Earth, has the characteristic that it teems with infinite fertility. If you were to get hold of part of this layer it would continually send forth new growth impulses. Rampant fertility is the intrinsic quality of this layer. Then we come to the sixth stratum, to the Fire Earth, which contains forces which can bring about terrible havoc and destruction. Actually, the primordial fire has been banished into these forces.

Ahriman's kingdom operates in a material sense in and from this stratum. What manifests in the phenomena of outer nature, in air and water, in cloud formations, in lightning and thunder—all this is, so to speak, a last vestige on the earth's surface of forces connected with ancient Saturn and which separated from the earth with the sun. Through the action of these forces, the inner fire-forces of the earth are placed in the service of Ahriman. He has his centre of activity here. Whereas his spiritual influences are drawn towards human souls in the ways described and lead them into error, we see how Ahriman—in a certain way shackled in chains—has certain foci for his activity in the interior of the earth. If we understand the mysterious connections of what has come to pass on the earth under Ahriman's influence and what Ahriman's own karma has become in consequence of this, we would recognize in earthquakes and earth tremors the connection between such grievous and tragic natural events and the power that holds sway on earth. These are manifestations of something which has remained behind on the earth since ancient times as a reaction against the good Beings of Light. Thus, various forces active on earth are connected with beings who were expelled from their connection with the earth when the good Beings of Light brought about beneficent phenomena around the earth. In a certain sense we can recognize the echos of these fire-forces, which in earlier times were withdrawn from human control, in what is wrought by fire in such terrible manifestations of nature. Although Ahriman's karma has been linked with human karma since the time of Atlantis, the suggestion should not arise that any guilt is to be attributed to those who are victims of what Ahriman's karma has evoked. Such occurrences are connected with the collective karma of humanity which individuals must also share. The *causes* which produce their effects in particular locations, as the working out of Ahriman's karma, often lie somewhere else entirely—while just these particular places afford the requisite opportunity.

We see there a connection which seems like a relic of catastrophes experienced by humanity in the far distant past. The power to work upon fire, which the human race once possessed in Lemurian times, was taken away from it. Ancient Lemuria was brought to its destruction by the fiery passions of human beings. The same fire that is below us now was above us then; it has receded from the earth's surface. The same fire that pours forth as a kind of extract from the primordial fire is the inorganic, mineral fire of today. So, too, the forces in air and water led to the Atlantean catastrophe, working again through human passions. These catastrophes were evoked by the collective karma of humanity. But a remnant has remained, and this remnant awakens echoes of those earlier catastrophes. Our volcanic eruptions and earthquakes are nothing else than the echoes of these catastrophes. It should never occur to anyone to attach an iota of guilt to the victims of such calamities or to withhold compassion in the fullest measure. It must be absolutely clear to an anthroposophist that the karma of these people has nothing to do with what he ought to do. It should never occur to anyone to withhold help from another because, to put it trivially, one believes in karma and, therefore, assumes that this destiny was brought on by the person himself. Karma demands of us that we help human beings because we may be certain that our help means that something is written in their karma which may turn it in a more favourable direction. Insight into the world based upon an understanding of karma must necessarily lead to compassion. Our compassion for the victims of such catastrophes will be all the greater, for our knowledge tells us that there is a collective human karma which its individual members are obliged to suffer. Just as such occurrences are brought about by humanity as a whole, so too must humanity be answerable for them as a whole. We must regard such a destiny as our own and help others not because we are free to volunteer to help, but because we know that we stand within the karma of humanity. What debts are to be paid are our debts as well.

A question was handed to me this morning about earthquakes. The question runs as follows: 'What is the occult explanation of earthquakes? Can they be foreseen? If particular catastrophes can be foreseen, why should it not be possible to give some warning beforehand? Such warnings might possibly be ineffective the first time, but certainly not a second time'.

Our older members may remember something that was said at the end of the lecture on 'The Interior of the Earth'[10] about the likelihood and occurrence of earthquakes. We will not consider that now but will enter directly into this question. In reality the question has two sides. One is whether earthquakes can be foreseen from the occult connections which can be observed. This question must be answered by saying that the knowledge of such matters belongs above all to the deepest realm of occult science. With respect to a particular terrestrial event, an event with roots as deeply laid as those described today and connected with causes extending widely over the earth, with respect to such an event it is absolutely correct to say that an indication of time *can* be given, even in a specific case. It would certainly be possible for the occultist to provide such a prediction. But now comes the other side of the question, whether it is *permissible* to give such predictions. For one who confronts occult secrets from the outside it will seem almost self-evident that the answer will be 'Yes'! And yet with regard to such events the truth is that a prediction can be made from the centres of initiation only two or three times a century—at the very most two or three times. For you have to remember that these things are connected with the karma of humanity as a whole. If these catastrophes were avoided in one instance they would inevitably occur in some other place in a different form. The prediction itself would alter nothing. Just think what a terrible interference into the whole karma of the earth it would be if human measures were adopted to prevent such occurrences. The reaction would be so fearful, so violent, that only in very rare and exceptional cases would a high initiate, foreseeing an earthquake, be able to make use of his knowledge to help himself or those near him. He would have to face his end *with full knowledge* and completely as a matter of course! For these things which have been woven into human karma for thousands and millions of years cannot be paralysed by measures adopted during one brief period of evolution. But there is still more to add.

It has been said that this very subject belongs to the most difficult occult investigations. As I said when I gave the lecture 'The Interior of the Earth', it is enormously difficult to know something about this interior. It is far easier to know something about the astral world, the devachanic world, even about the farthest planets, than about the interior of the earth. Most things one hears are the purest rubbish, because, as I say, it is one of the most difficult subjects in occultism. The same is true of things connected with these elemental catastrophes. You must realize above all that clairvoyance is not simply a matter of sitting down, inducing a particular state or condition, and then being able to say what is going on in the whole universe up to the highest spheres. That is by no means the case. Whoever believes that would think like someone who says: 'You are able to perceive the physical world. So why was it that when 12 o'clock came and you were sitting in your room, you were neither astonished by nor did you see what happened beside the River Spree at that hour?' There are hindrances to seership. If the seer in question had taken a walk at 12 o'clock he probably would have seen what happened. It is *not* the case that all worlds are immediately disclosed through the mere resolve to induce in oneself the requisite state of mind. The seer has to find his way to the events and investigate them, and investigations about the interior of the earth are the most difficult because the hindrances are the greatest. Perhaps at this point something may be said about these hindrances.

If a person is able to walk about on two legs, you can deprive them of this ability not only by amputating their legs but also by locking them up in a cell—then they cannot walk about. In the same way there are hindrances to occult research. In fact, in the realm we are speaking about they are powerful hindrances. I will offer one of the principal hindrances as an example and, in doing so, will introduce you to a mysterious relationship. The greatest hindrance to occult investigation in this realm consists in the methods and trends of modern materialistic science. The countless illusions and fallacies accumulating in materialistic science today, all the research that is not only futile, but is prompted by the vanities of human beings—these are things whose effects in the higher worlds make investigation into these phenomena and unimpeded vision in the higher worlds impossible, or to say the least, extremely difficult. Free vision is clouded as a result of the materialistic research pursued here on earth. One really cannot have an overview of these things without further considerations. I would like to say: just wait until the time comes when spiritual science has become more widespread and when, through its influence, the materialistic superstitions prevailing in our world will be swept away! Once the nonsensical analogies and hypotheses leading to all kinds of conjectures about the interior of the earth are cast aside, when spiritual science itself has been integrated into the karma of humanity, when it finds its way to human souls and is able to overcome the opposing powers and materialistic superstitions, when further research can be made into all that is connected with the bitterest foe of mankind, that being who chains man's vision to the sense world—then you will see that it will be possible, even externally, to influence human karma so that the dire consequences of such events may be alleviated. The reason why initiates must be silent about events connected with the great karma of humanity is found in the materialistic superstitions of human beings. Many scientific pursuits are not permeated with the Faustian striving for truth but are prompted entirely by vanity and ambition. How much scientific research is promoted in the world simply because an individual seeks his own personal advantage! If you add up all these things you will realize how strong the power is that obstructs vision into the world behind external sense phenomena. Not until this fog has been cleared away will the time come when, with respect to certain mysterious phenomena of nature emanating from the enemies of mankind and intervening deeply into human life, it will be possible for help to be given to mankind, and then in no small measure. Until that time comes no such possibility exists.

I am well aware that these questions have been given a turn not always found in the mind of the questioner. But it is often the fate of occult science to have to formulate questions in the right way before they can be answered correctly. Again, this does not mean that the mysterious connection between earthquakes and human karma is a secret that cannot be investigated. It *can* be investigated; but, there are reasons why only the most mundane aspects of such questions can be presented to the world today. Let the knowledge reach mankind through spiritual science that a connection exists between human action and events in nature. Then the time will come when humanity will wake up through this knowledge and these things can be answered in the way the questions demand. This time will come. For spiritual science may pass through many destinies. It may even happen that its influence will be crippled and remain within narrow and restricted circles. Nevertheless it will make its way through mankind and will be integrated into the karma of humanity. Then the possibility will be created for individuals themselves to have an effect upon human karma as a whole.

# II
# THE INTERIOR OF THE EARTH IN RELATION TO THE FORCES OF NATURE, WEATHER AND KARMA

# Forces of Nature, Volcanic Eruptions, Earthquakes and Epidemics in Relation to Karma (excerpt)

22 May 1910

What activities in earth existence can be described as regular, or normal? When our present solar system was organized in accordance with the goal of our earth, the regular motions of the earth and planets began. These terrestrial and planetary movements brought it about that the seasons of the year follow each other in regular succession, that we have sunshine and rain, that our fruits ripen in the fields, and so on. These conditions repeat themselves over and over according to the cosmic rhythms which shaped the present earth existence, after the Old Moon existence descended into twilight. But Lucifer works within earth existence. We shall see that he works a good deal more than merely in the realm outlined so far—in the human being himself—which he nevertheless has made his most important arena. Even if Lucifer were active only within earth existence, human beings would succumb to what we call 'luciferic temptations', not the least through the conditions created by the orderly course of the planets around the sun, the alternation of summer and winter, of rain and sunshine and so forth. If we were subject to everything which emanates from the order of the cosmos, everything generated by the regular rhythmical movements of the solar system, if only those laws appropriate to our present-day cosmos prevailed, we would be bound to succumb to Lucifer's influence, bound to develop a preference for the easy life over what we are supposed to attain for our cosmic salvation. We would be bound to prefer the predictable and regular course to what we ought to achieve for ourselves.

That is why counter-forces had to be created. Opposition forces had to be created by certain processes which interfere in the orderly cosmic processes of our terrestrial life. These were most beneficial and normal forces on the Old Moon, but today their activity on earth is abnormal and endangers the earth's orderly course. In a certain way these influences correct what would arise as an excessive inclination to a comfortable life, to ease and luxury, if only the rhythmical order prevailed. For example, such forces are manifest in violent hailstorms. So when what would otherwise be produced by the orderly forces of the earth is destroyed, a correction is brought about which, on the whole, works beneficially—even though people cannot see it at first, because a higher reason is at work than can be perceived by man. When hail drives down onto the fields, we can say that on the Old Moon the forces working in hail were the normal ones, just as are those which work beneficially today in rain and sunshine. But now the forces which work in hail rush in, in order to correct what is otherwise produced by the luciferic influence. And when the regular course is re-established, they rush in again to effect a further correction. Everything that leads to an ordered development belongs to the forces of the earth itself. When a volcano ejects lava, retarded forces are at work which have been brought over from the Old Moon to bring about a correction in earthly life. This applies, generally, to earthquakes and other phenomena involving the elements. Much of what comes from outside finds its justification in the general course of evolution. We shall see later on how this is connected with the human 'I'-consciousness. Many questions left open today will be addressed in that context.

But one point we must be clear on: these matters represent only one side of human existence, of earth existence, and of cosmic existence in general. If, on the one hand, we see the beneficial activity of spiritual powers in the destruction of an organ, and if we have found today that the whole course of earth evolution must be corrected by forces springing from the Old Moon existence, we have to ask: how it is that we earth people, on the other hand, have to try to rectify the harmful influence of the Old Moon forces? We already feel, as terrestrial man, that we have no right to wish for volcanic eruptions and earthquakes, nor may we ourselves destroy bodily organs to promote the beneficial effect of spiritual powers. But we can also say, and justifiably, that should an epidemic break out, it will lead man to look for the balancing of some imperfection within himself. And we can assume that we are driven into certain circumstances in order to suffer some injury whose overcoming will make us more perfect.

# Gravity, Volcanic Forces and Weather (excerpt)

26 November 1922

Let us discuss walking and its associated activities. I might describe walking as the process whereby man orientates himself within physical, earthly existence. When I move my arm or my hands, that too is related to the mechanics of walking; and when a tiny child begins to raise himself upright, that also is an act of orientation. All of this is connected with what is called the earth's force of gravity, with the fact that everything physical on the earth has *weight*. But one cannot say that the spirit-seed, which is built up between death and rebirth, has weight or heaviness.

Thus, everything connected with walking has to do with the force of gravity. Walking is, in fact, an overcoming of gravity. It is an act through which we place ourselves into the field of gravity. That is what happens every time we lift our legs to take a step forward. But we do not acquire this faculty until we are here on earth. It is not present in the life between death and rebirth, although something corresponds to it in that world. There, too, we have orientation, but it is not orientation within the field of gravity—for in the spiritual world there is no force of gravity, there is no weight. Orientation in that world is purely spiritual in character. Here on earth when we lift our legs to walk, we place ourselves in the field of gravity. The corresponding process in the spiritual world is becoming related to some member of the higher hierarchies, to an Angel for example, or an Archangel. A person feels himself inwardly near in soul to the influence of an Angel or an Exusiai with whom he is working. This is how one finds one's orientation in the life between death and rebirth. Just as here on earth we have to deal with weight, in the spiritual world we have to deal with what proceeds from individual hierarchic beings through forces sympathetic with our own human individuality.

The force of gravity has a single direction—towards the earth. But what corresponds to the force of gravity in the spiritual world operates in *all* directions, for the beings of the spiritual hierarchies are not centralized—they are everywhere. Orientation in the spiritual world is not geometric like the orientation of gravity towards the centre of the earth. Orientation in the spiritual world goes in all directions. According to whether a person has to build up his lungs or perform some other task with the beings of the hierarchies, they can say to themselves: the Third Hierarchy or First Hierarchy is pulling me in. He feels encompassed within the entire hierarchic world. He feels drawn to all sides not physically, as by the pull of gravity, but spiritually. In some cases he may feel repelled. This is what corresponds in the spiritual world to physical orientation within the sphere of terrestrial gravity.

★ ★ ★

Here on earth the universe has the rhythm proper and appropriate to mankind. In the spiritual world it has a rhythm which we ourselves take part in between death and rebirth. What, then, lies between the two? The rhythm proper to mankind gives us the faculty between birth and death to speak human words, to master human language. The cosmic rhythm enables us between death and rebirth to let the Cosmic Word resound within us. The earth endows us with the gift of speech. The spiritual universe gives us the Logos. As you might suspect, conditions where the cosmic rhythm gives us the Logos are utterly different from conditions here on the earth, where we articulate the human word in the air.

What, then, constitutes the boundary between one realm and the other? When we look out into the physical world we do not perceive the cosmic rhythm. An inner law and order exists in each realm, so what is it that lies between them? Between them, if I may put it so, is the boundary where the cosmic rhythm breaks in by coming too near the earth. Between them is what, in certain circumstances, may also bring the human respiratory rhythm into disorder. Between these two realms lie all the phenomena of *meteorology*. Without snow storms, blizzards, wind or cloud formations, if the atmosphere did not contain these meteorological phenomena, in addition to the oxygen and nitrogen required for breathing (which are always there, however clear the air may appear to be), we would look out into the universe and would be aware of a different rhythm. We would actually be aware of the counterpart of our breathing rhythm, only transformed into infinite grandeur. Between the two realms of the world order lie the chaotic phenomena of wind and weather, separating the cosmic rhythm and the human respiratory rhythm from each other.

In a similar fashion the earthly human being is subject to gravity. He co-ordinates his walk and every movement of his hands with the force of gravity. The forces are altogether different in the spiritual universe. Orientation there is in all directions; the lines of force run from being to being within the hierarchies. What is between the two? As meteorological phenomena lie between the heavenly rhythm and the human earthly rhythm, what lies between the cosmic force which is the opposite of gravity (orientation in all directions) and earthly gravity? Just as meteorological phenomena lie between the two rhythms, so between the force of gravity and the opposite heavenly force of orientation there lie *volcanic forces*, the forces which manifest in earthquakes. These are *irregular* or *erratic* forces.[1]

When viewed from the standpoint of the cosmos the forces working in the wind and weather are intimately connected with our breathing processes. Volcanic activity is connected with the forces of gravity so that it seems as though, from time to time, the supersensible powers are taking back fragments of the earth by interfering with the laws of gravity and casting into chaos what gravity has gradually built up, in order to take it back again. All earthly formations built up by the force of gravity are subject to these terrestrial phenomena. But whereas in the phenomena of weather the elements of air, warmth and water are active, in volcanic activity the solid and watery elements rise up in revolt. Here forces exist which lead beyond the normal laws of weight and gravity, and which in the course of time will do away with the earth, which itself originated out of the force of gravity.

Now, in addition to meteorological and volcanic forces there exists a third kind, which I shall speak about on another occasion.

★ ★ ★

In order to see the connections between these things we have to approach the spiritual. The moment we pass from the realm of ordinary natural law in one sphere—from gravity, for example—or from the rhythmic phenomena in the ether, the moment we pass from these into what is apparently chaos (although through this chaos we are led into higher realms of the cosmos) ... in other words, if we are to understand volcanic and meteorological phenomena, we *must* turn towards the spiritual.

Events in the world which appear to be purely accidental (for so they are called) are revealed in the spiritual realm in their fully lawful setting. One learns that between birth and death we are separated by meteorological phenomena from where we live between death and rebirth. If instead of the many abstractions current at the present time we are to speak concretely, we may say: in the heavenly regions the human being lives in a world order which is hidden from him on earth by the meteorological phenomena of the surrounding atmosphere. Meteorology is the dividing wall between what man experiences on earth and what he experiences between death and a new birth.

# Karma: Finding in Disaster the Path to Perfection (excerpt)

27 June 1924

Our discussions about karma can lead us only slowly and gradually to an understanding of this fundamental and complicated law. Today I would first of all like to refer to a fact, which must be emphasized, that in the elaboration of karma during the life between death and rebirth, cooperation exists primarily between those human beings who are living that life, in conditions I have previously described. We work together with people whom we are specially connected to by karma. Thus, we find karmically-connected groups of human beings working on their karma during the life between death and rebirth. It can truly be said that in this purely spiritual life clear differentiations exist between groups who are connected with one other. This does not preclude the fact that we also participate in the whole life of humanity and, above all, in the life of those who are incarnated on the earth. The fact that we belong to one particular group of souls does not exclude us from having an interest in humanity as a whole.

Yet, into all these groups of souls the activity of the beings of the higher hierarchies flows down right into the destiny of each individual. The higher hierarchies, who elaborate karma along with man during the life between death and rebirth, also work into our earthly life, where karma works itself out in the moral sense as destiny. Today, for once, we must find an answer to the question: how does the work of the hierarchies actually influence human life?

Speaking now with the help of initiation-science, one has to admit that this is a heart-rending and trenchant question. You can surmise from what I have told you in recent lectures that the phenomena of external nature are connected with the phenomena of human karma. Whoever looks not just at the immediate facts of nature, but also looks at the whole flow of cosmic and human events, perceives the connection between events which take place among different groups of people in one epoch and the phenomena of nature in another epoch. Sometimes we observe nature-events which break into earthly life. We witness devastating volcanic eruptions and observe what is brought about by the elemental forces of nature during floods or other similar phenomena.

If we regard such events as belonging merely to the natural order of things, we are confronted with something which is incomprehensible in relation to our general impression of the world. For here we observe events which simply break into the cosmic order, events which stand so contrary to what a person normally experiences that he gives up all hope of understanding them and simply accepts the bad luck they bring as a stroke of destiny. However, spiritual scientific research is able to take us a little further, for it opens up remarkable vistas precisely in connection with these elemental events of nature.

When we cast our eyes over the face of the earth we find that certain areas are literally covered with volcanoes. We find other parts of the earth which are prone to earthquakes or other catastrophes. If we examine the karmic connections of such events in the same way in which we have recently examined the previous connections of several historic personalities,[1] we arrive at some very peculiar results. We find the remarkable fact that up above in the spiritual worlds human souls live together in groups linked by their karma and work on their future karmic connections in accordance with the dictates of their past karma. What is more, we find that one karmically-connected group of human souls, while descending from pre-earthly into earthly existence, occasionally seeks out regions of volcanic activity or districts where earthquakes are prone to occur to receive their destiny from these elemental phenomena of nature. In the life between death and rebirth, where one's concepts and feelings are quite different, we find that such places are deliberately chosen by the souls thus karmically connected, in order to experience this very destiny. An idea which finds little enough understanding in our souls on earth is the following: 'I am choosing this great misfortune for myself in order to resolve my unfulfilled past karma'. As I have said, a decision like this, which finds so little understanding in earthly life, can be present in the life between death and rebirth as a completely justifiable one. We may deliberately seek out a volcanic eruption or an earthquake, to find in the path of disaster the path to perfection.

We must clearly distinguish between these two completely different outlooks upon life: one outlook from the spiritual world, and the other from the physical world.

But in this connection we have to ask ourselves something else. In the outer world, the everyday occurrences of nature proceed in an orderly fashion, for the starry worlds work with absolute predictability. This is above all the case with the sun and moon, indeed with all the stars, with the exception of the enigmatic phenomena of meteorites and comets which burst in upon the ordered, rhythmical occurrences of the cosmos in a remarkable way. However, what we call wind and weather, what interferes with the orderly course of nature, such as thunderstorms, hailstorms and other climatological and meteorological events—all these interrupt the daily rhythm of natural events. We see these things and, to begin with, resign ourselves to the outer course taken by natural phenomena. But later on, when the urge to understand spiritual things awakens within us, we listen to what is said by initiation-science, namely, that besides this outwardly visible world there also exists a supersensible world where the beings of the higher hierarchies dwell. And we enter the realm of these higher hierarchies in our life between death and rebirth, just as in our life between birth and death we live among the three kingdoms of nature—the mineral, plant and animal kingdoms.

We listen to what is taught by initiation-science and try to envisage the existence of this second world. But our thinking frequently stops short at this point, with the two worlds existing side by side without our connecting them together in thought.

We can only form a true idea of these two worlds when we can picture their existence simultaneously, and when with inner vision we realize the ways they work together and are interwoven. For this interworking must be thoroughly understood if we are to comprehend the shaping and forming of karma. Karma is prepared in the life between death and rebirth. But karma is also elaborated on earth with the help of the higher hierarchies who are active during our life between birth and death as well.

# III

# THE HUMAN BEING BETWEEN THE CELESTIAL AND SUBTERRANEAN SPHERES

# Memory and Conscience

LEADING LETTER 26

LEADING THOUGHTS 174–176

March 1925

While sleeping the human being surrenders himself up to the cosmos. He carries out what he has become as a result of his former earth lives. During his waking life the essence of his human nature is withdrawn from the cosmos. In this rhythm—surrender and withdrawal—human life takes its course between birth and death.

Withdrawal from the cosmos means at the same time that the soul-spiritual part of man is absorbed into the nerve-sense system. In waking life the soul-spiritual combines with the physical and life-processes of the nerve-sense system, so that they work together. In this united action, sense perception, the formation of memory and the play of imagination/fancy are contained. All these activities are bound to the physical body. The thinking experience, the process of conceptualization whereby one becomes *conscious* of what takes place semi-consciously in perception, imagination/fancy and memory—these activities are bound to the thinking organization.

The thinking organization, the region where man experiences self-consciousness, is an organization of the stars. If it lived and expressed *only itself* people would not have self-consciousness but a consciousness of the Divine. The thinking organization is lifted out of the starry cosmos and transplanted into the realm of earthly events. Man becomes self-conscious in that he experiences the starry worlds within the earthly realm.

Here the divine-spiritual world unites with part of man's inner life and sets him free so that he may become Man in the fullest sense of the word.

The divine-spiritual world lives on just beneath the thinking organization, where sense perception, the play of imagination/fancy and the formation of memory take place. The divine-spiritual lives in man's waking state in the unfolding of memory. The other two activities—sense perception and imagination/fancy—are only modifications of the processes which take place in the forming of memory pictures. In sense perception memory-content is formed at the moment of origination. In imagination/fancy a memory-content lights up which has been preserved within the soul's own being.

In sleep the soul-spiritual being of man is carried into the cosmic world. While asleep the activity of his astral body and ego is steeped in the divine-spiritual cosmos. He is not only outside the physical world but outside of the world of stars. Yet, he lives within the divine-spiritual beings who created him. At the present moment of cosmic evolution these divine-spiritual beings impress the moral content of the universe into the human astral body and ego during sleep. All of the world processes present in sleeping man are really moral processes and cannot be considered analogous to activities of nature.

Man carries over the after-effects of these processes from sleep into waking life, but the after-effects remain asleep in his will, since human beings are awake only in their thinking.

What takes place in his will is wrapped in darkness even while he is awake, just as his whole soul life is wrapped in darkness while he is asleep. But in this slumbering will-life the divine-spiritual works on in the waking life of man. A person is as morally good or bad as he can be according to how close he approaches divine-spiritual beings while he is asleep. And he comes nearer to them, or remains farther away, according to the moral qualities of his prior lives on earth.

What is implanted in the soul during sleep, while in communion with the divine-spiritual world, sounds forth from the depths of the waking soul as *the voice of conscience.* Thus, we see how the very things which materialism explains from mere natural causes have a moral source when viewed with spiritual knowledge. In *Memory* the divine-spiritual works directly within the waking human being. In *Conscience* the same divine-spiritual works indirectly in waking man as an after-effect. The forming of memory takes place in the nerve-sense organization. The forming of conscience takes place in the metabolic and limb-system, albeit purely as a soul-spiritual process.

Between these two lies the rhythmic system, whose activity is polarized in two directions. The rhythmic system, functioning as the breathing rhythm, is intimately connected to sense-perception and thought. It is at its most obvious in the breathing of the lungs. From there it grows finer and finer until, as a highly refined breathing process, it becomes sense-perception and thought. Sense-perception is still very close to breathing—it is a type of breathing, only through the sense organs, not through the lungs. Thought, or conceptualization, is further removed from the breathing of the lungs, and is upheld by the thinking organization.

What reveals itself in the play of imagination/fancy is

already very close to the rhythm of the circulation of the blood. It is a very inward breathing which comes into connection with the metabolic system and the limbs. Psychologically, too, the activity of imagination/fancy reaches down into the will, just as the circulatory system reaches down into the metabolic system and the limbs. In the activity of imagination/fancy thinking comes close to the will. Imagination/fancy is a diving down into that part of man's waking life which is asleep in the will. The contents of the soul of people who are especially developed in this direction appear like waking dreams. Goethe, who possessed such qualities, once said that Schiller had to interpret his own poetic dreams to him. Schiller, who had a different make-up, lived on the strength of what he brought with him from his previous incarnations. He had to reach within his powerful will for his imaginative content.

The ahrimanic power, in fostering its aims for the world, counts upon people who are especially developed in the sphere of imagination/fancy, who quite naturally transform their perception of sense reality into pictures of imaginative fancy. The ahrimanic power hopes to cut human evolution off from its past with the help of such people, and to steer it into the direction *it* wants for it.

The luciferic power counts on people who, while naturally more developed in their will, are inspired by an inner love for an idealistic world to transform their vision of sense reality into pictures of creative imagination. Through such people the luciferic power would like to keep human evolution completely confined within the impulses of the past. It would thus be able to keep mankind from diving down into the sphere where the ahrimanic power must be overcome.

Human beings are positioned on earth between two

opposite poles. Above us spread the stars which radiate forces connected with everything calculable and orderly in earth existence. The regular alternation of day and night, of the seasons and of the longer cosmic periods are earthly reflections of what takes place in the stars.

The other pole radiates out from the interior of the earth and what lives in it is chaotic. Wind and weather, thunder and lightning, earthquakes and volcanic eruptions—these are reflections of what takes place in the interior of the earth.

The human being himself is an image of this siderealterrestrial existence. In his thinking lives the order and regularity of the stars; in his will and limb system lives the chaos of the earth. In his rhythmic system he experiences his own earthly being in the free interplay and balance between the two.

The Goetheanum: February 1925

\* \* \*

Further Leading Thoughts issued from the Goetheanum for the Anthroposophical Society (with regard to the foregoing study on 'Memory and Conscience')

174. The human being is organized in body and spirit from two different sides. First, he is organized from the physical-etheric cosmos. What radiates from the divine-spiritual lives in human nature as the force of sense perception, the capacity for memory and the activity of imagination/fancy.

175. Second, the human being is organized from out of his own past lives on earth, which organization is comprised purely of soul and spirit and lives in his astral body and ego. Whatever enters into this part of human nature from the life

of the divine-spiritual lights up in him as the voice of conscience.

176. In his rhythmic system the human being experiences the constant union of the divine-spiritual impulses from these two sides. In the experience of rhythm the power of memory is carried into the life of will, and the power of conscience is carried into the life of ideas.

# From Nature to Sub-Nature

LEADING LETTER 29

LEADING THOUGHTS 183–185

March 1925

The Age of Philosophy is often said to have been superseded around the middle of the nineteenth century by the rising Age of *Natural Science*. It is also said that the Age of Natural Science continues in our day, although many people emphasize that we have found our way once again to certain philosophic pursuits.

All this is true of the paths of knowledge taken by the modern age, but not of its *paths of life*. The human being still lives with his concepts and ideas in Nature, in spite of the fact that he carries mechanical habits of thought into his theories of Nature. Yet he lives with his will-life in the mechanical processes of technology to such a far-reaching extent that the Age of Science has become imbued with an entirely new quality.

To understand human life we must look at it, to begin with, from two distinct sides. The human being brings with him from his previous earth lives the ability to think and conceive of the cosmic, which works inward from the spheres surrounding the earth and works within the earth domain itself. Through his senses he perceives the cosmic which works on the earth. Through his thinking organization he conceptualizes and thinks about the cosmic influences which work from the periphery downward to the earth.

Thus, the human being lives through his physical body in perception, and through his etheric body in thought.

What takes place in his astral body and ego governs the more hidden regions of his soul, for example, it governs his destiny. However, as a first step, we must look for these activities in the simple and elementary facts of life, not in the complicated relationships of destiny.

The human being is connected with certain telluric forces in which his entire organism is orientated. He learns to stand and to walk upright. He learns to place himself into the equilibrium of earthly forces with his arms and hands. These forces do *not* work inwardly from the cosmos; they are *purely* earthly forces.

In reality nothing a person experiences is an abstraction. People simply fail to perceive where the experience is coming from; and thus, they turn ideas about realities into abstractions. People talk about the laws of mechanics. They believe that they have abstracted them from relationships in Nature, but that is not the case. Everything a person experiences in his soul through purely mechanical laws has been discovered inwardly through his orientation to the terrestrial world (in standing, walking, etc.).

The mechanical is thus characterized as what is purely earthly. The natural laws and processes in colour and sound, for example, have entered the earthly realm from the cosmos. Only within the earthly realm do they, too, become permeated by the mechanical element. It is the same with the human being himself, who does not consciously meet with the mechanical until he enters the earthly realm.

By far the greater part of what works in today's technological culture, which is so intensely interwoven with human life, is *not Nature at all*, but is *Sub-Nature*. It is a world which emancipates itself from Nature—emancipates itself in a downward direction.

Observe how the Oriental, when he strives towards the spiritual, tries to free himself from the equilibrium of earthly forces. He assumes a meditative posture which returns him to a state of pure cosmic balance. In this posture the earth no longer influences the inner orientation of his body. (I am not recommending that you try this; it is mentioned merely to make our present subject clear. Anyone familiar with my writings knows how different the direction of Eastern spiritual life is from the Western.)

Humanity required this relationship to what is purely earthly in order to develop the consciousness soul. A strong tendency has most recently arisen to bring what is purely earthly, which humanity has to enter into for purposes of his evolution, into everything, even into the life of action. When a person enters into what is purely earthly he meets with the Ahrimanic realm. At this point he has to acquire a proper relationship to the Ahrimanic within his own being.

But the possibility of finding in this age of technology the right relationship to Ahrimanic civilization has escaped him until now. The human being has to find the inner strength of knowledge not to be overcome by Ahriman in this technological civilization. He must understand Sub-Nature for what it really is. He can only do this if he rises in spiritual knowledge at least as far into Super-Nature as he has descended in the technical sciences into Sub-Nature. The modern age requires a knowledge which transcends Nature, because it must come to grips in its inner life with a life-content which has sunk far beneath Nature—a life-content whose influence is perilous. Needless to say, there is no question of advocating a return to earlier conditions of civilization. The point is that people should find the way to bring the conditions of modern civilization into a proper relationship with themselves and with the cosmos.

There are, as yet, very few people who feel the significance of the spiritual tasks approaching humanity from this direction. Electricity, for instance, celebrated since its discovery as the very soul of Nature, must be recognized in its true character, in its peculiar power which leads down from Nature to Sub-Nature. People must beware lest they slide downward with it.

In the age before modern technology human beings found the spirit *within* their view of Nature. The technical processes now emancipated from Nature caused people to be mesmerized by the mechanical-material, which now became the genuinely scientific realm. All divine-spiritual being connected with the origin of human evolution is completely absent from the mechanical-material. The purely Ahrimanic dominates this realm.

In spiritual science we will create another realm where there is nothing Ahrimanic. Precisely by receiving spiritual knowledge, which Ahrimanic powers have no access to, are human beings given the strength to confront Ahriman *within the world*.

The Goetheanum: March 1925

\* \* \*

Further Leading Thoughts issued from the Goetheanum for the Anthroposophical Society (with regard to the foregoing study on 'Memory and Conscience')

183. In the age of natural science, since the middle of the nineteenth century, the activities of civilized humanity have been gradually sliding downward not just into the lowest regions of Nature, but even *below Nature*. Technology has become Sub-Nature.

184. This makes it urgent for humanity to develop a conscious experience of spiritual knowledge whereby it rises as high above Nature as it sinks beneath her in the Sub-Nature of technology. As a result man creates within himself the inner strength *not to go under*.

185. Earlier conceptions of Nature still contained spiritual qualities connected with human evolution, which have gradually disappeared altogether. Purely Ahrimanic spirituality has replaced it with our modern technological civilization.

# APPENDIX

# The Interior of the Earth

Adolf Arenson

In our reflections on the Sermon on the Mount we attempted to approach the New Testament scriptures in thought without detracting from their sanctity through our examination. We may have gained the impression that when we approach the subject in this way, we are able to reach a true appreciation of the treasures of wisdom and beauty lying dormant in those sacred books.

Let me turn to a subject from an absolutely different realm. Our present reflections will be occupied with descriptions from the spiritual investigator of the forces governing the interior of the earth, trying to bring his account more within our understanding. We know that the activity of these forces is malignant, and that they carry destruction and devastation into every domain of life. We also know that they influence our own nature to a remarkable degree, although we are unconscious of them in ordinary life. Therefore, we are justified in attempting to improve our acquaintance with these forces in a manner impossible by merely listening to the findings of occult research.

Since the day when a totally new understanding of the spiritual worlds and our relationship to them was opened up by the communications of the occultist, our relation to the world perceptible to the senses surrounding us has also changed. The idea that everything earthly is merely the expression of something spiritual may already have been familiar to us; but that idea was really a pure abstraction. It could not become a living reality until human and earthly evolution had been revealed by the graphic descriptions found in the numerous writings and lectures of Dr. Steiner which have appeared during the last ten years. We have risen from a general, vague conception of spirit to an under-standing of the living beings behind the events of the sense-perceptible world. Anyone who can free himself, even in a small degree, from the prejudices which unknowingly dom-inate people today will readily agree how little the present superficial thinking of mankind accords with the facts. The wonders of the world which meet us at every step are ascribed to the working of 'natural forces'. As if an abstract term like this could give us even a glimmer of knowledge! The occultist gives us examples of the inadequacy of such abstractions. What would we say in ordinary life if someone explained the workings of a watch by saying that it had been built by 'nature forces' which were still active in it. We would hardly be satisfied with such an explanation and would consider it nonsense. We know that every product of civilization comes into existence because a human being has invented and constructed it, and that every such object can ultimately be traced to an intelligence or a conscious being.

We have learned over the years to follow sound logic boldly to its consequences. When confronted by objects and events whose manifestation displays the 'pursuance of an aim,' we have learned to recognize that we can trace their ultimate cause to intelligences or conscious beings. Convinced of this, we have grasped the fact that nothing but knowledge of those beings and their activities makes it possible to gain a true understanding of the world we live in so that we may har-monize our own actions with the goal of evolution. Ample material has been provided for this purpose over the course of the decade. We have received information about the relationship of the higher worlds to the sense-perceptible world of facts from the most varied realms of spiritual and terrestrial events.

These communications often appear at first to be without apparent connection to one another. Sometimes they even offer direct contradictions—open contradictions. But we have learned that the apparently missing links actually exist, and that all contradictions are synthesized into a higher harmony. We found that our work consists of tracing these links and solving these contradictions through our own efforts.

While pursuing this plan of study we had the following remarkable experience. When we succeeded in duly collecting and arranging the materials given to us, these connecting links jumped out at us as if by themselves, and the contradictions were resolved effortlessly. Along with this experience a new conviction arose, that the way these communications were made was itself a powerful educative factor. By following up these connections and solving the contradictions ourselves, we transform the disclosures of the occultist into our own knowledge. Without such knowledge acquired by our own work, all the wisdom proclaimed to us would be of little value. We would remain theorists without the power to exercise a healthy influence on our lives. With self-won knowledge we make ourselves fit to undertake the mission allotted to us in universal evolution, for whose fulfilment we are being prepared and educated by the occultist.

Please consider the following exposition from that point of view. Its intention is to help bring within our reach a subject which, perhaps more than any other, is difficult to understand.

In 1906 a course of lectures was given by Dr. Steiner in Stuttgart,[1] where a picture of both planetary and human evolution was unveiled for the first time. These lectures are a classical example of the way theosophical conceptions of the world should be introduced. All the so-called introductory courses delivered since then by students of theosophy are based on this course. Now, while nearly everything in the course described a gradual process of evolution, from the nature of the human being to the different methods of initiation, the last lecture contained something quite new and unexpected: a description of the interior of the earth. In the closing lecture we were told that the earth is not as modern natural science assumes it is, a huge, lifeless ball, the same inside and outside, the only difference being that the substances on the inside are in a fluid condition. We were told that our earth is composed to its centre of a series of strata differing from one another, but all of which cannot be compared with any substance on the earth's surface. These strata were then briefly characterized. We did not understand this description at the time, and could only wait patiently in the hope that other lectures might follow to help us to arrive at an understanding of the subject. A few lectures were actually delivered on earthquakes and volcanic eruptions where the strata of the earth were mentioned. Some details were even added, but the further explanation we had hoped for was never given.

However, seven years have elapsed since that first communication, and we are in possession of materials which make a more thorough study of the subject possible. I am permitted to draw upon this material and, by its judicious arrangement, allowed to shed light on the descriptions originally given. It will thus be necessary to recall what was said regarding those subterranean strata. We cannot do so in detail, but we can bring out what is characteristic of each stratum in a few pregnant words.

The uppermost stratum, which is like an eggshell to an egg, is called the Mineral Earth. Below it lies the so-called Fluid Earth which is not fluid in a physical sense. Its substance begins to have spiritual qualities, since when brought into contact with anything living it immediately expels and annihilates that life. The third stratum, the Vapour Earth, turns a sensation into its opposite. The existing form of the sensation is extinguished, just as life is extinguished by the second stratum. The fourth layer, the Water or Form Earth, consists of a substance which materializes everything that happens spiritually in devachan. We find there the negative images of physical objects; for example, a cube of salt here would be destroyed, but its negative would arise. This layer is the fount of everything that exists as matter on the earth. The fifth stratum, the Seed or Growth Earth, teems with exuberant growing force. It provides the life behind the forms of the fourth layer. The next stratum is the Fire Earth. It has sensation and will and it consists entirely of passions. It is the vehicle of everything in the nature of desire, the fount of all animal pleasure and pain. The next stratum is the Earth Reflector. It transforms all qualities into their opposites; everything one imagines as morality in human nature is here changed into its opposite. Then follows the Explosive Earth which splits everything up, including moral qualities. Strife arises on the earth's surface through the forces this stratum radiates. The primary cause of all disharmony lies here. All destruction of form is prepared here. Finally comes the Earth Core through whose influence black magic arises in the world. Spiritual evil goes forth from this part of the earth.

This description, taken from various lectures, provides the characteristics of each strata. It remains for us to shed light on these descriptions, so that new facts may find their place in what we already know about the cosmos and our planet. With this aim let us endeavour to group together the materials available to us. It is important—we have already emphasized this fact—that we should call to mind the words of the occultist about this subject. A saying which may serve here as a key runs somewhat as follows:

'When one force begins to work in the universe another force, opposed to the first, arises at the same moment. Everything that happens in the world is subject to the law of polarity'.

We can well understand this saying, for even in ordinary thought we observe something of this kind. For instance, we could never form the concept 'good' if the opposite concept 'evil' were not known to us. The same may be said of 'large' and 'small', 'long' and 'short'. In every case one concept implies its opposite. Polarity exists everywhere, even in our thoughts. On this basis we may make the following reflection. Although we cannot understand the forces in the interior of the earth, nevertheless we can try to find those forces in the universe which are opposed to them, which we know with certainty exist in accordance with the law of polarity. Perhaps we may understand these polaric forces better—they are possibly already well known to us—so that through their help we may learn to understand the unknown forces in the interior of the earth.

An intellectual task like this cannot be recounted in all its phases. Our thoughts do not simply take a straight line. But if we described the fruit of our study in its essentials, it might be as follows. We recall the description of the genesis of a solar system given in the Düsseldorf² course in 1909. From that picture we see primal forces stirring in the Trinity; the plan is brought forth. Exalted beings receive it and carry it out in wisdom; new forces begin to work. The Thrones or Spirits of Will offer up their substance which becomes the outer manifestation of the plan of the Universe. Ever new beings cast their forces into the world-process. The earth evolves into ever new conditions, until at last we reach the epoch when the human being shuts himself off within his skin and achieves Ego-consciousness.

These good, progressive forces endowed man with everything he needed to fulfill his earthly mission. Now we know that with the first stirring of the progressive forces, at the same time the activity of opposition forces began. While we may try to understand the beings who have overseen humanity's progressive evolution, it also becomes our duty to ask about their antagonists who send out destructive forces of annihilation and obstruct the normal evolution of the human race. Where are these beings and forces to be found? Where should we look for them? They work outwards from the interior of the earth. Figuratively we might say: 'As the earth cooled and solidified, these forces fled into the earth; they were, so to speak, banished within the earth'. This figure of speech it is quite legitimate if we compare the activity of the chthonic forces with the benefits lavished upon us by the progressive beings from the higher worlds. Let us place these dual activities side by side: one on the one hand and one on the other.

Consider the first stratum, the Mineral Earth, which is the scene of human evolution at the present epoch. Which beneficial forces are most closely connected with this stratum? Which influence it most directly? The vital forces at work in our etheric or life body influence it most directly. The formless, lifeless mineral becomes endowed with form and life when the vital forces become associated with it. Life arises wherever these vital forces unite with lifeless substance. What type of forces work against these? They must be such that whenever they meet anything living, they drive out and destroy that life. Let us look again at how the second stratum, the Fluid Earth, is described: 'The Fluid Earth, when brought into contact with anything living, immediately drives out and destroys life'.

Let us continue. The forces which exert an influence on what is alive make sensation possible. The plant lacks sensation, because these forces are not present in it; but it is otherwise with animals, which are endowed with sensation, with forces that permit the flashing-up of sensation. What are we told about the third stratum or Vapour Earth, which is the corresponding polarity to the forces of sensation? 'Its substance turns sensation into its opposite. We might say that here sensation is extinguished, however it exists, just as life is extinguished by the second stratum.' These two examples already show us that we are on the right track. Let us now proceed to the next higher level.

So far we have only considered the Mineral Earth and the two realms which bestow life and sensation. But just as the mineral is penetrated with life, and life is permeated with sensation, sensation is in its turn penetrated by thought. We know from the findings of occult research that every manifestation on the earth's surface corresponds to something spiritual. The archetypes are their spiritual counterpart and are found in the 'Spiritland'. In *Theosophy*,[3] we are told that the Spiritland is woven out of the same substance as human thoughts. We find various 'regions' in this Spiritland. First come the three regions of Lower Devachan: the Continental region containing the archetypes of all that is purely physical; the Oceanic region, with the archetypes of life; and the Atmospheric region, with the archetypes of sensation.

Having advanced in our study to the regions whence the spiritual archetypes send out their forces, it is our task to examine whether the forces active in those regions correspond to the others which develop their pernicious activity from the interior of the earth. We begin with the first region of the Spiritland, the archetypes of everything physical, remembering that these archetypes are spiritual. The empty spaces seen by the clairvoyant in the Spiritland in place of the objects and beings 'when they manifest physically are filled, to a certain extent, with physical substance'.

To understand what this means we must make a short digression. In the lecture course *From Jesus to Christ*,[4] we are told that the true physical body is invisible because it is a body of forces. What we perceive with our senses are the physical substances which fill out this invisible body. We see mineral substances filling this body; the body itself is invisible. This amounts to saying that the present physical body of man, as it has been changed by Lucifer's influence, really consists of two different elements. It is composed of the spiritual archetype from the first region of the Spiritland and the lower 'filling' incorporated into it. Now we understand what is meant when we are told that the fourth layer, the Form Earth, which corresponds to the first region of the Spiritland, is the fount of all 'matter' or 'substance' on the earth. Here we have two poles: in the Spiritland are the spiritual archetypes of the physical body; in the Form Earth are the primal astral forces of the lower physical element, 'densified to physical substance on the first layer, the surface of the earth', as described in the lecture noted.

In the second region of the Spiritland the archetypes of life stream through the spiritual world as a liquid element, forming a unity—the creative primal forces for all beings endowed with life that appear in the physical world. What do we find in the fifth stratum, in the Seed, or Growth Earth? Here, too, we find life, but the kind of life which gives the fourth stratum its characteristic rank growth: 'The Seed Earth abounds in exuberant teeming energy; it serves as the life underlying the forms of the fourth stratum'.

The forces which work downward from the third region of Spiritland stand in a similar relationship to those which originate in the sixth layer, the Fire Earth. The archetypes of everything pertaining to the soul are found in their spiritual aspect in the Spiritland. In the sixth layer of the interior of the earth are found all passions of a low nature. This region is the vehicle for all impulses of desire and is the source of animal pleasure and pain.

Then comes the fourth region of the Spiritland which contains the archetypes of all purely creative works, including the spiritual archetypes of everything specifically human. Now, what can we designate as specifically human? What is its highest form of expression? What, we may ask, is peculiar to the human being, and only to the human being, as opposed to the other kingdoms of Nature? His moral feelings, his moral thoughts. Morality is a quality possessed only by human beings. Look at what is said about the corresponding chthonic layer—the Earth Reflector: 'Its substance changes everything into its opposite; everything we can imagine as morality in human nature is here transformed into its opposite'.

Higher still, in the loftiest regions of the Spiritland, forces are active which do not manifest in form. Hence this region is called 'Arupa'—meaning formless, without shape. These are the creative forces of the archetypes themselves, living germs which take form as thought-entities in the lower regions of the Spiritland. We find forces of the opposite pole in the eighth subterranean layer, where powers work against the former. The source of all strife, all discord on earth, is found here. In the Spiritland the impulses towards the archetypes are 'ready to assume the most manifold forms of thought-entities'. Here 'all form-destroying elements are prepared in substance'.

Finally we come to the last and highest to which our thoughts can rise, which is still closed to our understanding, and which we therefore vaguely call the 'First Cause', 'Primeval Womb' and the 'Godhead'. When we are told that the germinal thought-entities in the highest regions of Spiritland envelop the actual seed of life, but that the seed comes from still higher worlds, we faintly divine that from those higher worlds the first stimulus is given to all that directs growth and watches beneficently over evolution. We have a name for this; we call it 'white magic'. The lofty spiritual force which guides and protects the evolution of the earth originates here. The 'Earth Core' forms the counterforce to this: 'Through its influence black magic arises; the force of spiritual evil proceeds from this region'.

We have pointed out the connections between the forces in the interior of the earth and the ruling powers in the cosmos. Not that we have gained any understanding of the nature of these forces, but we have assigned a place in the world organism to what formerly seemed isolated and disconnected. And we have done something else. What we recognized as truth remains our own knowledge; we can never forget it. Even if we should forget the names of the different strata or forget the details, one essential thing can never be extinguished. When we are struck by the activity of the progressive deities in any connection whatever, a picture of the powers of hindrance who send out their forces from the various strata in the interior of the earth will rise up. As our comprehension of the guidance of the good powers dawns upon us, so do we understand better the work of those beings who obstruct the normal course of evolution, who seemingly destroy and annihilate it, but who, precisely because of their antagonistic energy, call forth as if by enchantment the most hidden capacities and forces of the human soul.

Something else becomes clear, namely, the fundamental basis of the activity of the beings in the interior of the earth. Here our understanding unfolds only gradually. It is no new foreign element as compared with the activities of the good gods. Although it contrasts to the latter, it still lies on the same line of advance. But it oversteps its limits and is turned into a low force—dragged into the abyss. While good gods lead us with protecting care into the world of matter so that the human form may be built up, the activity of the obstructive beings overstrains these forces. These beings drag matter down to a withering, parched state of obduracy, parched callosity. While life is showered upon us from spiritual worlds, the energies from the interior of the earth degenerate into rank growth. While we are endowed by the good spirits with the capacity for sensation and feeling, this is exaggerated into its opposite as lust and animal desire. And while the possibility of freedom has been bestowed upon man, who is privileged to experience the isolation of the 'I', the Ego, the downward-tending powers strive to tempt selfhood beyond its limits into conflict, into the 'war of all against all'.

We find another association when we consider the strata of the interior of the earth with respect to the peculiar activity of each one and come to the following conclusions. The Mineral Earth represents lower substantiality. The Fluid Earth represents the life-extinguishing stratum; it has to do with life. The Atmospheric Earth, which extinguishes sensation, has to do with feeling. These three form a trinity which corresponds to the trinity of the human body: the physical body, etheric body and the body of sensation.

Then follow: the Form Earth, the primal source of all substantiality; the Seed Earth, the primal source of all lower life; and, the Fire Earth, composed entirely of lower passions. Again we find a trinity of substance, life and feeling. These correspond in man to the sentient soul, the intellectual soul and the consciousness soul which, according to the second lecture in *Rosicrucian Wisdom*,[5] are transformations of the physical body, etheric body and the body of sensation. Finally we have the Earth Reflector, the Explosive Earth and the Earth Core. These direct their energy not only against matter, life and feeling, but also wage war against the spiritual elements of morality, harmony and white magic. Corresponding to these are the principles of man's higher nature: the Spirit-Self, Life-Spirit and Spirit-Man.

It is evident that we are presented here with connections which, if pursued further, might lead us into profound mysteries of human nature. But in this brief lecture we must restrict ourselves to an outline and can only hint at these things today. For another question forces itself upon us when we observe the workings of the law of polarity in the world-process—a question which may fill us with apprehension, but which we cannot push away, because it affects the central point of evolution.

If every progressive force produces an opposing force, and if obstructive forces immediately place themselves in opposition to all beneficial activities, what is the end of it all? What is the ultimate goal? Where lies redemption? To approach this question more closely, let us again recall what the world-process really signifies in its deepest sense.

We see spiritual beings and forces at work, showering gifts of the most varied objects and abilities upon man, so that he may be equal to the task allotted to him. They have endowed him with the principles of his nature which enable him to live in the physical world. They have bestowed upon him the capacity of thought, and ultimately, of self-consciousness, so that he is poised to become an independent being in the further course of evolution. (The occultist endeavours to make those spiritual beings more understandable by describing their characteristic qualities.) On the other hand, we see other beings at work who are antagonistic to them. As we have seen, every group of higher beings is opposed by a corresponding group in the interior of the earth.

In the middle, so to speak—for this requires a spatial image—is the surface of the earth, the mineral plane, that region where the collision takes place between these opposing forces. For on the earth's surface a being has gradually developed who is the product of this polarity. Man is appointed by the good gods to turn the experiences of earth to account for the benefit of the spiritual worlds. If nothing had counteracted the forces of the good gods, man would have become a being without any personal will, acting only at the command of the good gods. But the destructive beings stand opposed to the progressive deeds of the good gods.

Both groups direct their energies towards the human soul where their encounter takes place.

Here we arrive at an important truth: the forces of polarity work through the human soul, the lowest as well as the highest. Christ Himself works through the human soul when He fulfills the mission of the human race. He would spiritualize and redeem the physical world. The human soul must take the Christ-Force into itself so that the work of redemption may be accomplished. The soul can fill itself with the Christ-Force, or it can turn away from it. Therefore, as the arena where the encounter between the forces from above and below takes place, everything depends on how the soul develops itself. For from the shock of the collision between these opposing forces, a spark may leap forth which changes someone into a free divine being who consciously absorbs the highest forces into himself in order to accomplish the work of redemption.

We begin to understand the task allotted to the human being in the plan of the Universe from yet another perspective. Since the earth began, forces have been working from above and from below, conditioning one another in their polarity. With every new force arises its counterforce—the struggle seems endless. In the middle between the two a being is developing, a being who absorbs the forces that assail him from both sides. On one side and on the other stand the opposing powers; in the middle is man. And man, with the help of Christ, raises himself in freedom step by step. As he permeates himself with the forces of the higher regions, he conquers and redeems the regions below him. Man must reconcile the polarities which created him. The meaning of evolution is placed before us in a picture accessible to human thought and understanding. Through man the world-polarities are harmonized so that a new, creative, cosmic activity may arise.

But how can this be achieved? We have already expressly stated that this can only be done with the help of Christ. This is more emphatically confirmed by the words of the occultist when he tells us that every single step in Christian initiation, the Washing of the Feet, the Scourging, the Crowning with Thorns, etc., leads to the conquest of a corresponding layer in the interior of the earth. This means that the experiences of Christian initiation signify a penetration into the interior of the earth. This may point the way for us.

If through Christ's strength we are given the ability to redeem the forces in the interior of the earth, we must look for the words where He shows us the way, where He tells us how we can follow that way. Building on all that we have heard from the occult teacher let us try to find them.

In a lecture on planetary evolution the occultist presents us with a picture of the future.[6] Man will now master the vital forces which once awakened life and form in the lifeless mineral layer without his help. As man has begun to master the mineral realm, as he is already able to create a work of art or a machine out of lifeless matter, so in the distant future he will have the ability to cause life to arise at will—and not by planting a seed in the earth—for he will then be a creator of life.

But to this end he must evolve from the physical towards the spiritual. To become lord of the mineral kingdom and to subject terrestrial substance to his own will, he was forced to turn his attention towards the earth, to cut himself off from the spiritual, to direct his thoughts and interests to the earth and to grow attached to the physical plane. He must now leave it of his own free will and turn again towards the spiritual. For the life-giving forces hold sway there, forces he must unite with in order to redeem those beings who extinguish life. The yearning for spiritual life, corresponding to the true core of his being, must be so strong that he is ready to renounce everything the earth has to give. This yearning is the key which opens up the spiritual realms to him—the Kingdom of Heaven. Here we see the link between spiritual research and the words of Christ: 'Blessed are the beggars for the spirit, for theirs is the Kingdom of Heaven'.

Then the force will arise in him to unite himself with the beings who have bestowed sensation upon us. Beings linger in the Vapour Earth who send up forces to extinguish sensation. To conquer them man must learn to absorb and master forces of sensation of every kind. He must learn to bear the most powerful feelings, even the greatest sorrow, if he would hold his own in the struggle with those beings. This is a tremendous task. Man will not be able to fulfil it unless he is supported by the spiritual comfort which he derives from the knowledge that at every step upon this path he is preparing himself more and more to become the liberator of the powers striving downwards: 'Blessed are those who mourn, for they shall be comforted'.

But whoever would vanquish lower substantiality, whose source is in the next layer, the Form or Water Earth, must unite himself with the forces ruling the first region of the Spiritland. We know that entry into the Spiritland demands a mighty exertion of will. From the descriptions of the afterlife given by the occultist we know that, when a person is compelled in accordance with law into the spiritual world, everything binding him to the earth, all the unconquered desires that still have hold of him, must first fall away. To conquer this fourth stratum he has to transform his lower passions into equanimity of soul through his own free will. Only in this way can he succeed in wresting from Ahriman what he now possesses, for Ahriman is the ruler of the lower substantiality. Thus, if man wishes to master the lower substantiality of the earth in order to spiritualize it, he must attain a state of gentleness, of equanimity: 'Blessed are the meek, for they shall inherit the earth'.

And so man strides forward to the second region of the Spiritland, the Oceanic, where he experiences the unity of all life. He must steep himself in the forces of this region if he would battle with the beings who serve as life to the lower substantiality. He acquires here a new and higher understanding of the laws that work in karma. Now he knows that the law of destiny does not merely signify reward and punishment, but serves to uplift humanity towards the unity of all life. He recognizes the regulating, compensating force which provides a way out of the chaos of separate life, and he longs with all his soul for unity among men. From this ardent longing new forces will be born which he can victoriously oppose against the dark powers of earth. His yearning, his desire, will become a force of conquest: 'Blessed are those who hunger and thirst after righteousness, for they shall be filled'.

He then reaches the third region of the Spiritland, the Atmospheric, where a stand can be taken against the beings of the Fire Earth. The Fire Earth contains everything pertaining to desire and consists entirely of low passions. To redeem them he has to draw forces from the spiritual archetypes of the soul-nature, which will enable him to lose himself in the joys and sorrows of every creature. Whoever would overcome the primal source of lower passions must outgrow his own. He must be able to empathize with the feelings of others and pour love into the souls of his fellow men: 'Blessed are the merciful, for they shall obtain mercy'.

Thus at every stage man must conquer new forces in order to achieve his work of deliverance. In the seventh layer he meets those beings who try to destroy all that represents the flower of human soul evolution—the feeling for divine purity, the striving after moral perfection. From the beings inhabiting the fourth region of Spiritland he can derive the strength to conquer here too. With the help of those forces, his heart, the expression of his 'I', can steep itself in moral perfection so that, beholding God, it can live and act in purity: 'Blessed are the pure in heart, for they shall see God'.

In such hearts the peace of God will abide. To wage war against the Explosive Earth, the first cause of all strife, a person must have harmonized the discord in his own soul: 'Blessed are the peacemakers, for they shall be called the children of God'.

Such people have prepared themselves to make the last sacrifice. The force of spiritual evil issues from the Earth Core and through its influence black magic arises. Man redeems the heart of the earth by offering himself up and becoming one with God: 'Blessed are those who are persecuted for righteousness' sake, for theirs is the Kingdom of Heaven'.

In the lecture on the Sermon on the Mount[7] we find spiritual connections between the Gospel of St Matthew and the Gospel of St John. Here, in our consideration of the interior of the earth, a new agreement comes to light. The report of the spiritual investigator accords with the words the Redeemer spoke two thousand years ago.

These connections were not the fruit of a laborious search; they seemed to grow out of the words themselves. Whoever meditates upon the Sermon on the Mount in conjunction with the message of the occultist experiences that connections like these meet him at every turn. They are indeed present, only they evade the superficial glance.

The purpose of my lecture was to call attention again to the method of study recommended by the occultist. In Dr Steiner's *Theosophy* you will find words of strength for such work : 'Thought is a living force: it is a direct expression of what is beheld in spirit'.

Whoever truly understands these words also grasps the truth, that the communications of the spiritual teacher may be to us what outer Nature is to the natural man—it created him; it sustains him. The spiritual spring flowing into our souls must create and sustain the true man within us. But to this end our thinking must be transformed. It has been kindled in the world of lower passions and is itself low, as long as it serves desire. It must purify itself and offer itself up as a sacrifice. This is the path thinking has to follow. We stand upon its threshold. But when after tireless striving we succeed in purifying ourselves, when thought is transformed into an offering, a sacrificial flame, it will, like an earthly flame, annihilate the lower element which kindled it, to which it owes its origin, and will soar aloft to spiritual heights.

# Esoteric Conversations

Excerpt from a memoir by
COUNTESS JOHANNA KEYSERLINGK

The challenge had been given to us during the Agricultural Course[1] to place a spiritual science alongside the science of the universities, as a contribution towards overcoming the ever more threatening rise of materialism. ...

There is something more to it than the mere forging of Michael's Sword. It is a fact that in the occult regions of the earth, what is prepared by the forging of Michael's Sword is carried to a subterranean Altar in the process—to an Altar which is invisible and which really exists beneath the earth.

To become acquainted with nature forces under the earth, to get to know the divine being working in nature, leads to an understanding of the fact that the Michael Sword, in the process of being forged, is really carried to an Altar under the earth. The dead take part in this. It has to be found by sensitive souls. It is necessary that you get involved and work together so that more and more souls find the Michael Sword. Nothing is accomplished by the mere forging of the Sword. It only becomes effective when it is found. Be strong and modest in your self-assurance that, as young people, you are called by destiny to seek for Michael's Sword, to find it and carry it out into the world.

★ ★ ★

At the close of the lecture[2] Rudolf Steiner walked round the circle to say goodbye. He went to each one and not only gave them his hand, but took every hand that was offered him in both of his, as though sealing a bond with them. It was like a solemn commitment to a soul pledge of faithfulness to serve the spiritual tasks of our time.

We did not suspect at the time that this handshake was, for most of us, a leave-taking from him for the rest of our lives.

These words were spoken to the young people because it is they who have forces for the future, impulses which penetrate into the soul and at the same time into the interior of the earth. For one's own inner being is also the interior of the earth into which we can all penetrate. In this way the Altar will be found by following the path and teaching of St John. Rudolf Steiner made this appeal many times and one can truthfully say that the Anthroposophical Society was on the point of failure through neglect of this advice. It is not head-forces but heart-forces fructified from the depths which will be able to lead us out of the present crisis.

According to Rudolf Steiner it is, therefore, not only a matter of developing the forces of iron within us, but of penetrating down into the depths of the soul, to the ground of the world where the Altar stands in objective reality. The forging of the Sword and the placing of it on the subterranean Altar was the deed of Michael working with the dead—but finding it must be done by the living.

It requires courage and truthfulness to pierce the depths of one's own soul world. There one encounters the Apocalyptic Beasts. The abyss of one's own soul darkness is revealed—and human beings are afraid of that. 'It is fear' Rudolf Steiner once proclaimed, 'which prevents man from penetrating into his own soul depths!' If this warning had been heeded a true Rosicrucianism would have been able to oppose the storm of materialism because, being deeply anchored in the fundament of the soul, it would have been linked together with the Godhead. People prefer, however, to persuade themselves that a command of material life is the most important thing. One therefore drowns the call of one's own soul which sounds a warning from the depths—and one stays on the surface. Frau von Moltke once said to Rudolf Steiner: 'People are unable to penetrate into the depths!' 'No,' said Rudolf Steiner decisively, 'they do not want to'. Man's will has become free—he is able to decide for himself which direction to take. The agricultural lectures were thus given a solemn ending.

Rudolf Steiner had the kindness to come up to my room, where he spoke to me about the kingdom in the interior of the earth. We know that at the moment when Christ's blood flowed down on to the earth at Golgotha a new sun-globe was born in the earth's interior. My search had always been directed to the study of the earth's depth, for I had seen a golden kernel light up within the earth—named by Ptolemy[3] the primeval sun. These golden depths I could only connect with that land which Rudolf Steiner said had been hidden from the sight of man, and that Christ would open the gates in order to lead those who seek for it to the submerged fairy-tale land of Shambhalla, of which the Indians dream.

What I had experienced had been so real—and yet I did not want to lapse into fantasies. I had written down my questions. Rudolf Steiner read them aloud: 'Where can we find the land Shambhalla? I can imagine it somewhat as follows: in the beginning there was fire and light. These took their strength from one another—reciprocally in complete harmony. Then the light rejected the forces of fire; and the smoke, which was thereby hindered from rising into the light, fought back and accumulated above the fire. Thus, the primeval fire was gradually covered over by the ashes from the smoke. The ashes from the primeval fire form the mineral part of our earth'.

Rudolf Steiner reflected for a moment: 'That is interesting!' Then he continued to read aloud: 'First of all people could see through to their original homeland, the primal sun, but the earth became ever more dense—smoke increasingly darkened their view of the primal sun. Man appeared to be separated by a mineral layer from the primal sun, which is paradise, the land which was lost from the sight of earthly eyes, but from which man originated. The kernel of the earth consists of golden fire, around which a dark girdle is cast, the smoke of the mineral realm'.

Rudolf Steiner paused once more: 'What you have written is correct', then he continued to read: 'We human beings, however, have to rediscover the connection to our origin, otherwise we shall become more and more excluded from life and will solidify with the minerals of the earth. If my assumption is correct we must start to penetrate the depths to the golden ground of the world. The way leads through the darkness, through the layers of smoke which envelop the living fire. The earth-layers of the mineral world are permeated with the kamaloka of our soul life'.

'Yes, that is correct,' said Rudolf Steiner, who continued to read: 'There we meet with everything which connects the mineral darkness to the hell of souls. When we step out of the human world—which can occur even while the body continues to exist on earth—then we arrive in the land of the dead. When the dead person has accomplished his kamaloka, he rises to the starry worlds. I would think, though, that if it were possible to achieve a state of sinlessness in kamaloka and, instead of rising upwards, one were to remain in the depths, would not the golden gates of the realm of fairyland open once more for the petitioning soul?'

Rudolf Steiner added: 'Yes, that is possible'.

I: 'And is the interior of the earth made out of that gold which comes from the hollow cavity in the sun and which is destined to return there'?

Rudolf Steiner: 'Yes, the interior of the earth is of gold'.

Then he put down the paper. Still I continued to question him for my assurance.

'Herr Doctor, when I am standing here on earth', and I pointed to my green carpet, 'then the golden land is beneath me, deep in the interior of the earth—and if I now attain to sinlessness and remain in the depths, the demons will not be able to harm me and I will be able to penetrate beyond them—and reach the golden land?'

Rudolf Steiner: 'If one passes through them accompanied by Christ, the demons will not be able to harm you—but otherwise they would indeed be able to destroy you'! He added emphatically: 'They can, however, become our helpers. Yes, that is so—the path is a true one, but it is very difficult'! I knew now that my investigation had been on the right lines, but this path was a 'very difficult' one.

It was Hölderlin[4] who had shown me his path. For years his astral forces had led me. I had climbed after him through the depths of fire and death until he found the way out to the light, the way out of imprisonment. He, who even left the earth in order to search for the Gods, '. . . for to be alone and without the Gods was death to him', knows the Christ in the depths. So he does not rise up to the stars as other dead people do. No, he prefers to penetrate to the depths, to the Sun Being at the centre of the earth.

The indication by Rudolf Steiner that what I had seen was

the truth, but 'very difficult', left me wondering, and it seemed to me that he meant that there was a different way for the pupils of Michael. Now it has been granted, through the help of Michael, that the Christ who appears in the etheric realm of the earth will illumine our eyes to see the lost magical land. Then this land will rise up to us and man will bond himself to a new world-day in the light of the sun, when he sets free from their enchantment the spirits of the elements who have darkened his vision and rendered the earth solid and opaque.

In Rudolf Steiner's Mystery Drama *The Guardian of the Threshold*[5] Ahriman says: 'The gods, however, willed to rule on earth, and from their kingdom they did one day thrust my power into the depths of the abyss ... and thus 'tis only from this place I dare send out my powerful strength upon the earth. But in this way my power turns into fear'. And Capesius calls out: 'Oh, in the depths dark fear is threatening'! The spirit-pupil must, therefore, be aware of the fact that whoever penetrates into the depths has to pass through Ahriman's kingdom, and the beings of that kingdom touch him!

As well as thinking and feeling the Being of Christ who united with the earth through His death, one must also strive to become a brother of the divine Christ in order to attain in a full and living way the rays of victory which await us beyond the darkness. The spirit-pupil thereby gains a weapon to protect him: the reality and power of perceptive consciousness! Perception of the laws of light is the shield which, in the hour of danger, is ready at hand. The spirit-pupil who would dare to journey on the road into the depths must be in possession of that knowledge which ensures victory through Christ.

I then asked Rudolf Steiner if we would always be exposed to destruction by the demons: if they always have to destroy everything or whether we can be taken into the protection of Christ. He replied: 'When we have entered into the circle of the sun the demons will no longer be able to harm us'.

My next question was also related to the primeval depths. I asked him what substance kept the primeval fire alight, for where there is fire there must first be substance, and so the primeval fire is not the beginning which produces original life out of itself. Rudolf Steiner replied: 'No, it is different—it is not so in this case. On earth there has to be material for fire to burn. But the primeval fire burns spontaneously; it is its own substance and being! Substance only came later and was added to the Fire'.

I: 'Then is the primeval sun of Ptolemy, which he perceived in the centre of the earth as the creative ground of the world, the golden fairyland Shambhalla'?

Rudolf Steiner: 'Yes—and midnight conceals it'.

Then I presented Rudolf Steiner with the diagram [over] and asked: 'Can one draw it like this'? He answered: 'Yes, one can do that'.

'The festivals', I said, 'are always at the points where a new spiritual current enters in and relieves an old one. The Father is succeeded by the Son and the latter is succeeded by the powers of the Holy Spirit'. Rudolf Steiner then asked me what I called the three uppermost points and I answered that they were to be assigned to Easter, Pentecost and St John's Day. Then I stopped because I did not know what to call the lower point on the right and the one at the bottom. He pointed to the lowest apex: 'What do you call this'?

'The journey of Faust to the Mothers', I answered.

'Yes', said Rudolf Steiner, 'on November 9', and added:

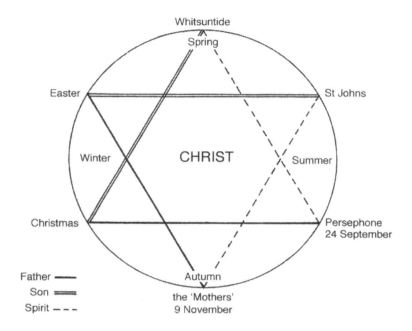

'And here, on 24 September, the Festival of Persephone[6] was celebrated by the Greeks'.

I then put several questions connected to what had been spoken about during the last few days, and which could not be separated from it in my view. I only wish to recount a few of these questions here, ones which might provide confirmation to one or other of us who are investigating these things further. Rudolf Steiner asked me if I had any further questions and I showed him my calculations in astronomy and voiced my opinion as follows: 'A completely new astronomy is developing which has nothing at all to do with what one calls astronomy today. I do not dare to work further on that until I know if what I am writing is true'.

Rudolf Steiner: 'If you experience these things as you have, then they will be true. You only have to be quite sure in yourself, quite selflessly true'. And, only audible to spirit ears, he added: 'Because these truths can only be experienced in selflessness'.

I: 'You told me Christ is the Divine Ego. So is the earth the physical body of Christ, the etheric world His etheric body and the astral world His astral body?'

Rudolf Steiner: 'Yes, of course'.

I: 'I see many things but, without having asked you, I surely cannot say, for instance, that in the slag of cooled moon craters the dead fire-forces of God's adversaries are crouching and wrangling with Him'?

Rudolf Steiner: 'Why do you not like to say so, if you experience it in that way'?

★ ★ ★

When Rudolf Steiner was with us the previous time he had said something which has occupied me a great deal, since here on earth one can close an inner door, but in the spiritual world it is different: 'On Sirius one hears everything that people think'. I studied all I could find to gain a grasp of the identity of Sirius. Mythology only revealed that it was the star of Zarathustra, and stands as Isis in the constellation of the Dog. Neither did the Astronomical Course[7] give me any information about the secrets of Sirius. Then I thought that I should tackle this question from a different angle and formulated it according to my own ideas as follows: Where is the centre in which all human suffering and all human joy in heaven and in the cosmos can be perceived? Then the answer sounded in my soul: it is His heart—the heart of Jesus—Zarathustra in the earth depths of midnight. I asked Rudolf Steiner about this and he said: 'Sirius is the heart of Jesus-Zarathustra and is in the depths of the earth'.

'The heart is the deep', said Jacob Boehme: in the depths of his heart man also attains to the other Heart, which would bear with him all his suffering and all his joy. Then Rudolf Steiner drew a simple sketch and spoke slowly for me to take it down in writing: 'Sirius is the world-thought which Christ produces out of His Heart—therefore it is to be found within the earth'. He drew a curve to represent the earth and wrote on it, 'Metabolism and fulfilment', as though the thoughts issuing from the Heart of Christ, that is from the sun, are sent through Sirius to the centre of the earth, where they obtain their fulfilment by means of metabolism.

\* \* \*

Rudolf Steiner also spoke to me at that time about 'Creation out of nothing'. I noted down the following: the interior of the earth consists of gold, in which the highest hierarchy weaves. This interior became dark: and Christ departed from the sun and, as the Saviour, entered the golden centre of the earth. So is this new Creation a gift to the earth out of nothingness, out of the hollow space within the sun? For the solid earth—this body of the Gods—died at the moment of Golgotha. Has a new Holy Host now been sent down from the hollow space of the sun?

Rudolf Steiner answered: 'Not out of the hollowness, for that is "nothingness" isn't it, the opposite of "something-ness". The new Holy Host issues forth from the reality behind the emptiness'.

I: 'And will the mineral slag of the divine corpse become the vessel which begins to shine? Will all the mineral parts of the earth shine—or will a part of it remain behind, dark and unredeemed'?

Rudolf Steiner: 'All substance will be redeemed'. I then

asked if the moons of the planets will also be redeemed and he answered: 'They are the refuse, yet they will also be redeemed—all substance will be redeemed'.

I: 'Is there any waste matter apart from the moons'? Rudolf Steiner: 'Yes, that will remain, but later on that too will be redeemed'. And then, with great seriousness: 'If everything were not to be redeemed, that would mean that Ahriman would have triumphed. All substance will gradually be redeemed after a very long time. If anything should be lost, then Ahriman would be the victor'!

I said: 'I am also looking for the relationship of the Demiourgos (world-creator) to Ahriman'. He replied: 'The Demiourgos is, so to say, the young Ahriman'.

I: 'His building material is the mineral'? Rudolf Steiner nodded and I continued: 'And when the Demiourgos meets the Christ will this mineral then become the Holy Grail'?

Rudolf Steiner: 'Yes, that is correct'.

# Notes

### Foreword
1. Temple Lodge Publishing 2005.
2. Both quotes from the lecture of 16 April 1906.
3. Lecture of 21 April 1906.
4. Also published in English as *Anthroposophical Leading Thoughts*.
5. *The Philosophy of Freedom, Christianity as Mystical Fact, Theosophy, Knowledge of the Higher Worlds* and *Occult Science*.
6. For this and the prior quote see lecture of 4 September 1906.
7. Temple Lodge Publishing 1999.

### The Interior of the Earth and Volcanic Eruptions
1. Founded by Pythagorus, a Greek philosopher and mathematician who lived in the 6th century BC.
2. The Lemurian epoch is the third of seven evolutionary epochs of earth evolution. The Lemurian continent, situated in the present location of the Indian Ocean between Australia, India and Africa, ended in a cataclysmic fire catastrophe. See Rudolf Steiner's *Occult Science*, Chapter Four.
3. The Atlantean epoch, the fourth of the seven evolutionary epochs of earth evolution, is dated tentatively by Wachsmuth as ending in 7,227 BC. Atlantis, situated in the Atlantic Ocean between present-day Europe and North America, ended in a water catastrophe known in the Bible and many native traditions as the Flood.

**The Interior of the Earth**

1. Since its famous eruption in AD 79 Mount Vesuvius has erupted about once every hundred years. It entered a 600-year period of inactivity in AD 1037, not erupting again until AD 1631.
2. Charlemagne (AD 742–AD 814).
3. Frederick the Great (1712–1786).
4. This period lasted approximately 1,000 years.

**Rosicrucian Training, The Interior of the Earth, Earthquakes and Volcanoes**

1. Dante Alighieri (1265 AD–1321 AD), Florentine poet whose finest work *The Divine Comedy* is considered the greatest literary work of the Middle Ages. It contains poetic descriptions of the various layers of the Subterranean Spheres, characterized as 'levels of Hell'.

**Mephistopheles and Earthquakes**

1. Referencing Goethe's *Faust: Part Two* wherein Faust pursues the ideal feminine in the guise of Helen of Troy into a spiritual realm outside of space and time deep within the earth known as the Realm of the Mothers. See Steiner's lecture of 12 March 1909 (Berlin), 'Goethe's Secret Revelation and The Riddle of Faust'.
2. *Faust*, Part Two, 'A Gloomy Gallery'.
3. Ibid.
4. Book of Job: 6–12
5. *Cosmic Memory: Prehistory of Earth and Man* by Rudolf Steiner (Massachusetts: SteinerBooks, 2006).
6. Golgotha, the Greek name of the hill upon which Christ was crucified, is known in Roman Catholicism as Mount Calvary. The 'Event of Golgotha' is alternatively described by Rudolf Steiner as the 'Mystery of Golgotha' and comprises the crucifixion, death and resurrection of Jesus Christ.

7. After the destruction of Atlantis in the Flood a number of the inhabitants migrated east to the region of the Gobi Desert, there to set forth the new impulse for the Post-Atlantean Epoch, which has seven Cultural Ages. We are currently in the fifth Post-Atlantean Cultural Age, which runs 1413 AD–3573 AD. The preceding four Post-Atlantean Cultural Ages were the Indian (7,227 BC–5,067 BC); Persian (5,067 BC–2,907 BC); Egypto-Chaldean (2,907 BC–747 BC); and Greco-Roman (747 BC–1413 AD).
8. *Faust*, Part Two, 'A Gloomy Gallery'.
9. Alternative names for the Asuras used by Steiner are the Archai or the Spirits of Personality.
10. Referencing the lecture of 21 April 1906 contained in this volume.

### Gravity, Volcanic Forces and Weather

1. At this point in the lecture Steiner refers to a report alleging that Easter Island has been destroyed by a terrible earthquake. The report was later found to be incorrect.

### Karma: Finding in Disaster the Path to Perfection

1. Steiner is referring here to the series of lectures published as *Karmic Relationships Vols. I–VIII* (Sussex: Rudolf Steiner Press).

### Appendix: The Interior of the Earth

1. *At the Gates of Spiritual Science*, GA 95; also published as *Founding a Science of the Spirit* (Rudolf Steiner Press, 1995).
2. *The Spiritual Hierarchies and their Reflection in the Physical World*, Anthroposophic Press, 1996.
3. Rudolf Steiner, *Theosophy: Introduction to the Supersensible Knowledge of the World and the Destiny of Man* (Rudolf Steiner Press, 1995).

4. Rudolf Steiner, *From Jesus to Christ* (Rudolf Steiner Press, 1995).
5. Rudolf Steiner, *Rosicrucian Wisdom* (previously published as *Theosophy of the Rosicrucian*) (Rudolf Steiner Press, 1995).
6. At time of publication it has not be possible to trace the lecture Wachsmuth is referring to.
7. See *The Ten Commandments and the Sermon on the Mount* (New York: Anthroposophic Press, 1978).

**Appendix: Esoteric Conversations**
1. Keyserlingk is referring to the course by Rudolf Steiner on biodynamic agriculture, given at Koberwitz in June 1924. See *Agriculture Course* (Sussex: Rudolf Steiner Press, 2004).
2. This is Steiner s lecture of 17 June 1924 entitled *Youth's Search in Nature* which is not published as part of the Agriculture Course but was given in Koberwitz the day after it ended. It is found in GA 260a. (The reference to the subterranean Michael Altar begins on page 285.) The full German title of the lecture is *Jugendansprache wahrend der Brealau-Koberwitz Tagung uber die Weg der verlorengegangen wirksamen Krafter der Natur.* ('Address to the youth during the Breslau-Koberwitz conference concerning the path of the lost vitality of the powers of nature.')
3. Ptolemy (*c.* 90–168 AD): astronomer, mathematician and geographer who lived in Alexandria, Egypt. Author of the astronomical treatise the *Almagest*, the geographical study *Geography* and the *Tetrabiblios*, which endeavoured to adapt horoscopic astrology to Aristotelian natural philosophy.
4. Friedrich Holderlin (1770–1843), a major German lyric poet whose work formed a bridge between the Classical and Romantic schools.
5. Rudolf Steiner, *Four Mystery Dramas* (Rudolf Steiner Press, 1995).
6. Persephone (Proserpina in Roman mythology), known as the

Queen of the Underworld, was the daughter of Demeter and Zeus who was abducted by Hades, the god of the Underworld, but was rescued by her mother Demeter. Persephone thereafter had to spend four months of each year in the Underworld. She is connected with the mystery centre at Eleusis. See also Rudolf Steiner's *Wonders of the World, Ordeals of the Soul, Trials of the Spirit* (GA 129) (London: Rudolf Steiner Press, 1983).

7. See *The Relationship of the Diverse Branches of Natural Science to Astronomy* (Rudolf Steiner Research Foundation, 1989).

# Sources

1. 16 April 1906, 'The Interior of the Earth and Volcanic Eruptions', published in *Original Impulses for the Science of the Spirit* (Lower Beachmont, Australia: Completion Press, 2001), GA 96, Lecture II (excerpt). Trsl. A.R. Meuss.
2. 21 April 1906, 'The Interior of the Earth', contained in the cycle *Das christliche Mysterium* (*The Christian Mystery*) (Dornach: Rudolf Steiner Verlag, 1998), GA 97, Lecture 27.
3. 12 June 1906, 'Earthquakes, Volcanoes and the Human Will', published in *An Esoteric Cosmology* (New York: Spiritual Science Library, 1987), GA 94, Lecture 16 (excerpt). Trsl. R. Querido.
4. 4 September 1906, 'Rosicrucian Training, The Interior of the Earth, Earthquakes and Volcanoes', published in *At the Gates of Spiritual Science* (London: Rudolf Steiner Press, 1986), GA 95, Lecture 14 (excerpt). (Formerly published as *At the Gates of Theosophy* and recently published as *Founding a Science of the Spirit*, London: Rudolf Steiner Press.) Trsl. E.H.G. & C.D.
5. 1 January 1909, 'Mephistopheles and Earthquakes', published in *The Deed of Christ and the Opposing Spiritual Powers* (London: Rudolf Steiner Publishing, 1954), GA 107. Trsl. D.S. Osmond.
6. 22 May 1910, 'Forces of Nature, Volcanic Eruptions, Earthquakes and Epidemics in Relation to Karma', published in *Manifestations of Karma* (London: Rudolf Steiner Press, 2000), GA 120, Lecture 7 (excerpt).
7. 26 November 1922, 'Gravity, Volcanic Forces and Weather', published in *Man And The World of Stars* (New York:

Anthroposophic Press, 1963), GA 219, Lecture 1 (excerpt). Trsl. D.S. Osmond.

8. 27 June 1924, published in *Karmic Relationships*, Vol. II (London: Rudolf Steiner Press, 1974), GA 236, Lecture XV (excerpt). Trsl. M. Cotterell, C. Davy & D.S. Osmond.

9. March 1925, 'Memory and Conscience'; Leading Letter 26, Leading Thoughts 174–176; published in *Anthroposophical Leading Thoughts* (London: Rudolf Steiner Press, 1973). Trsl. G. & M. Adams.

10. March 1925, 'From Nature to Sub-Nature'; Leading Letter 29, Leading Thoughts 183–185; published in *Anthroposophical Leading Thoughts* (London: Rudolf Steiner Press, 1973). Trsl. G. & M. Adams.

**Appendix:**

1. 'The Interior of the Earth', Adolf Arenson (1914). Published previously as *The Interior of the Earth* (London/New York: Rudolf Steiner Publishing/Anthroposophic Press, 1914).

2. 'Esoteric Conversations', excerpt from a memoir of Countess Johanna Keyserlingk (1924). Published previously in *The Birth of a New Agriculture* (London: Temple Lodge Publishing, 1999), GA 327. Trsl. J.M. Wood.

# A NOTE FROM RUDOLF STEINER PRESS

We are an independent publisher and registered charity (non-profit organisation) dedicated to making available the work of Rudolf Steiner in English translation. We care a great deal about the content of our books and have hundreds of titles available – as printed books, ebooks and in audio formats.

## As a publisher devoted to anthroposophy...

🔄 We continually commission translations of previously unpublished works by Rudolf Steiner and invest in re-translating, editing and improving our editions.

🔄 We are committed to making anthroposophy available to all by publishing introductory books as well as contemporary research.

🔄 Our new print editions and ebooks are carefully checked and proofread for accuracy, and converted into all formats for all platforms.

🔄 Our translations are officially authorised by Rudolf Steiner's estate in Dornach, Switzerland, to whom we pay royalties on sales, thus assisting their critical work.

So, look out for Rudolf Steiner Press as a mark of quality and support us today by buying our books, or contact us should you wish to sponsor specific titles or to support the charity with a gift or legacy.

office@rudolfsteinerpress.com
Join our e-mailing list at www.rudolfsteinerpress.com

🔄 RUDOLF STEINER PRESS